Published by Rails-to-Trails Conservancy
Ohio Field Office
30 Liberty Street
Canal Winchester, Ohio 43110
(614) 837-6782
rtcohio@railtrails.org

Rhonda Border-Boose and Annemarie Holmes

ISBN# 0-9721782-1-X

Front Cover: Front Cover: Knox County, Mohican Valley Trail, Bridge of Dreams. This trail may be found on page 126.

Guide designed by:

PRINTED AND ELECTRONIC COMMUNICATIONS
www.kunocreative.com
600 BROADWAY   LORAIN, OH   (440) 245-2801

Contents

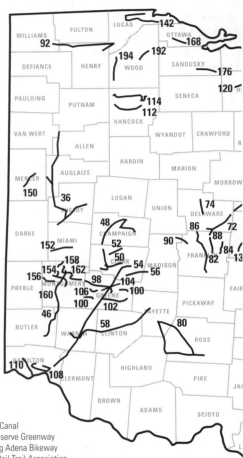

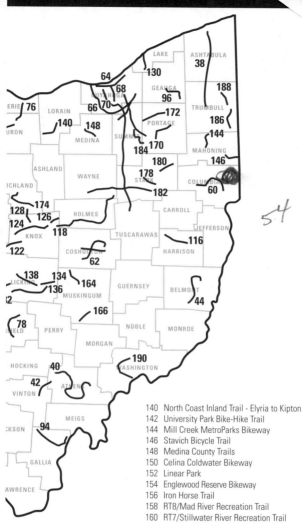

Contents - By County

Contents - By County

Trail Index

Athens Bicycle
14 West Stimson Avenue
Athens, OH 45701
740-594-9944
866-594-9944
pete@athensbicycle.com
www.athensbicycle.com

Baer Wheels
3030 North High Street
Columbus, OH 43202
614-267-7178
www.baerwheels.com

Baker BJ Bicycle Sales
996 W. Prospect Road
Ashtabula, OH 44004
440-997-3486

Barn Inn
6838 C.R. 203
Millersburg, OH 44654
877-674-7600
www.bbonline.com/oh/thebarn

Best Bike Shop
78 Lexington Avenue
Mansfield, OH 44907
419-522-3696

Bicycle Boulevard
20132 Chagrin Boulevard
Shaker Heights, OH 44122
216-751-2583
sirbike@aol.com

Bicycle One
82 Mill Street
Gahanna, OH 43230
614-478-7777

Bicycle Stop
1355 West 1st Street
Springfield, OH 45504
937-342-4780
www.bicyclestop.com

Bike Source
2887 North High Street
Columbus, OH 43202
614-267-1387
www.bikesourceline.com

Bike Source
4840 Sawmill Road
Columbus, OH 43235
614-459-1200
www.bikesourceline.com

Bike Source
591 South State Street
Westerville, OH 43081
614-891-6280
www.bikesourceline.com

Bike Route, The
5201 Monroe Street
Toledo, OH 43623
419-885-3030

Bike Warehouse
5445 Bethel Sawmill Center
Columbus, OH 43235
614-761-7777

Bikewise
11 West Church Street
Oxford, OH 45056
513-523-4880

Bikeworks
5631 Alexis Road
Sylvania, OH 43560
419-882-0800

Breakaway Cycling
17 West William Street
Delaware, OH 43015
740-363-3232
1-888-234-BIKE
custombike@juno.com
www.custombike.com

Canal House Bed & Breakfast
Mary and Joe Shurilla, Innkeepers
306 South Canal Street
Canal Fulton, OH 44614
330-854-6229
888-875-2021
mainstay@cannet.com

Century Cycles
33351 Aurora Road, RT 43
Solon, OH 44139
440-519-0013
info@centruycycle.com

Century Cycles
1079 North Court Street (RT 42)
Medina, OH 44256
330-722-7119
medina@centrycycles.com

Century Cycles
19955 Detroit Road
Rocky River, OH 44116
440-356-5705
river@centurycycles.com

Century Cycles
1621 Main Street (Route 303)
Peninsula, OH 44264
330-657-2209
peninsula@centruycycles.com

Cycle Path, Inc.
104 West Union Street
Athens, OH 45701
740-593-8482
path@frognet.net
www.athenscyclepath.com

Cycle Sales Co.
7394 Market Street
Youngstown, OH 44512
330-758-8090

Eddy's Bike Shop
3707 Darrow Road
Stow, OH 44224
330-688-5521 or 330-688-6920
info@eddys.com
www.eddys.com

Eddy's Bike Shop
3991 Medina Road
Montrose, OH 44333
330-666-2453
info@eddys.com
www.eddys.com

Eddy's Bike Shop
2830 Bishop Road
Willoughby Hills, OH 44092
440-943-2453
info@eddys.com
www.eddys.com

Eddy's Bike Shop
25140 Lorain Road
North Olmstead, OH 44070
440-779-1096
info@eddys.com
www.eddys.com

Ernies Bike Shop
135 Lake Avenue
Massillon, OH 44647
1-800-291-0099
ernie@erniesbikeshop.com
www.erniesbikeshop.com

Ernies Bike Shop
1325 Portage Street NW
North Canton, OH 44720
330-494-5323
ernie@erniesbikeshop.com
www.erniesbikeshop.com

Ernies Bike Shop
315 Wabash Avenue NW
New Philadelphia, OH 44663
330-343-4056
ernie@erniesbikeshop.com
www.erniesbikeshop.com

Ernies Bike Shop
340 East Liberty Street
Wooster, OH 44691
330-262-9003
ernie@erniesbikeshop.com
www.erniesbikeshop.com

Five Rivers MetroParks
Craig Wenner
1375 Sibenthaler Avenue
Dayton, OH 45414
937-278-8231
cwenner@metroparks.org
www.metroparks.org

Fox's Pizza Den at Trail View Plaza
Tom Bryan
42 North Grant Street
Millersburg, OH 44654
330-674-1369
eat@foxpizza.com

Fremont Cycle & Fitness Center
107 N. Ohio Avenue
Fremont, OH 43420
419-332-4481
waggswheels@gliss.cc

Hearthstone Inn and Suites
Stuart and Ruth Zaharek
10 South Main Street
Cedarville, OH 45314
937-766-3000
877-OHIO-INN (644-6466)
www.hearthstone-inn.com

Inn at Honey Run
6920 County Road 203
Millersburg, OH 44654
800-468-6639
www.innathoneyrun.com

K&G Bike Center
116 West Franklin Street
Dayton, OH 45459
937-436-2222
kgdout@aol.com
www.kgbikes.com

K&G Bike Center
4090 Marshall Road
Kettering, OH 45429
937-294-6895
kgdout@aol.com
www.kgbikes.com

K&G Bike Center
594 North Detroit Street
Xenia, OH 45385
937-372-2555
kgdout@aol.com
www.kgbikes.com

Kettering Bike Shop
3120 Wilmington Pike
Dayton, OH 45429
937-293-3293
937-339-1634

Loveland Bike and Skate Rental
Martin Schickel
206 Railroad Avenue
Loveland, OH 45140
513-683-0468
martinschickel@fuse.net
www.lovelandbiketrail.com

Mainstay B&B
Mary and Joe Shurilla, Innkeepers
1320 East Main Street
Louisville, OH 44641
330-875-2021; 330-854-6229
888-875-2021
mainstay@cannet.com

Mill Creek MetroParks
P. O. Box 596
Canfield, OH 44406
330-702-3000

Ohio Environmental Council
1207 Grandview Avenue, Room 201
Columbus, OH 43212
614-487-7506

Ohio Greenways
2179 Everett Road
Peninsula, OH 44264
330-657-2055
info@ohiogreenways.org

Ohio Parks and Recreation Association
1069-A Main Street
Westerville, OH 43081
614-895-2222
www.opraonline.org

Olde World Cyclery
5545 North Ridge Route 20
Madison, OH 44057
440-428-9854
savagewebb@lightstream.net

Orrville Cycling and Fitness
9658 West High Street
Orrville, OH 44667
330-682-1911
www.orrvillebikeshop.com

REM Cycles
8529 Mentor Avenue
Mentor, OH 44060
440-255-6294

**Robert M. Martin - Wachovia
Securities** 65 East State Street,
13th Floor
Columbus, OH 43215
800-848-0211

Second Chances Bicycles, LTD
1324 Duncan Avenue
Cincinnati, OH 45208
513-871-5814

Southside Cycling
2924 Maysville Pike
Zanesville, OH 43701
740-453-7550

StudioTemple
Velma Esprit Garnes
265 Lincoln Circle, Studio B
Gahanna, OH 43230
614-337-0368
www.studiotemple.com

SurfNCycle
150 West Mound Street
South Charleston, OH 45368
937-462-SURF (7873)
www.members.aol.com/
Andrew4244/

The Porch House B&B
Bruce and Lisa Westall, Innkeepers
241 East Maple Street
Granville, OH 43023
740-587-1995
porchhouse@porchhouse.com
www.porchhouse.com

Trek Bicycle Store
2720 Sawmill Place Blvd.
Columbus, OH 43235
614-791-8735
www.trekstorecolumbus.com

Victoria Green Plains Farm - B&B
Austin and Sarah Wildman
8606 Selma Pike
P. O. Box 393
South Charleston, OH 45368
937-462-8682
wildman@greenplain.com
www.greenplain.com

Village Cyclery
110 Dayton Street
Yellow Springs, OH 45387
937-767-9330
vilcyclery@aol.com

Werseil's Bike & Ski Shop
2860 West Central
Toledo, OH 43606
419-474-7412

West Chester Cyclery
9304 Cincinnati Columbus Road SR 42
Cincinnati, OH 45241
513-777-8020
wccylcery@aol.com

City of Wilmington Parks
and Recreation Department
69 North South Street
Wilmington, OH 45177
937-382-4781
www.ci.wilmington.oh.us

Y Not Cycling & Fitness
2188 West Fourth Street
Mansfield, OH 44906
419-747-6087
ynotbike@earthlink.net

Y Not Cycling & Fitness
64 East Main Street
Lexington, OH 44904
419-884-6135
ynotbike@earthlink.net

Y Not Cycling & Fitness
133 South Main Street
Mt. Vernon, OH 43050
740-392-6100
ynotbike@earthlink.net

Young's Jersey Dairy
6880 Springfield-Xenia Road
Yellow Springs, OH 45387
937-325-0629
cows@youngsdairy.com
www.youngsdairy.com

Acknowledgements

This book is dedicated to all those who believe that trails and greenways improve our quality of life and who work to bring the dream alive in Ohio and across the country, for this generation and all who will follow.

The Ohio field office would like to thank all those who worked to make this book a reality. We would especially like to thank the following individual and corporate sponsors for their support of rail-trails in Ohio:

Bricker & Eckler LLP

Cardinal Health

Five Rivers MetroParks

Stephen Gray

The GUND Foundation of Cleveland

H. T. Mead Foundation

Richard Housh

Louise H. and David Ingalls Foundation

Gene Markley

Mill Creek MetroParks, Mahoning County

National Park Service

Don Noble

Noble Foundation

Ohio Environmental Council

Ohio Greenways

Ohio Parks and Recreation Association

Justin Ristau

Robert Rogan Burchenal Foundation

Marcia Sauer

Jim Schneider

StudioTemple

Ellen Tripp

Wachovia Securities, Inc. – Robert M. Martin

Charles H. Waterman III

City of Wilmington Parks and Recreation

Young's Jersey Dairy

A special thank you to the members of the Rails-to-Trails Conservancy Ohio Advisory Board for their continued support of the Ohio field office:

Amy Bowman-Moore

Chris Copeland

Susan Dicken

Stephen Gray

Rich Housh

Paul Labovitz

Gene Markley

Robert Martin

Don Noble

Matt Ogle

Justin Ristau

Marcia Sauer

Jim Schneider

Jack Shaner

Charles H. Waterman III

a member of **Earth Share**
OF OHIO

For 19 years Rails-to-Trails Conservancy (RTC), in cooperation with citizen groups, public agencies, railroads, and other industries, has facilitated the conversion of over 15,000 miles of former railroad corridors into recreational public trails in all fifty states. Headquartered in Washington D.C., RTC has regional offices in the Northeast, Midwest, Southeast, and West Coast. Each office works with dozens of groups throughout the region to provide assistance and technical support in organizing trail systems crossing counties, states, and the country. RTC utilizes existing canal towpaths, riparian corridors, greenways, utility corridors, mass transit lines, walking paths, and bike trails to connect communities and encourage economic growth. Several hundred miles of rail-trails are already operational in Ohio, and nearly a thousand more are in various stages of development.

RTC is a daily witness to both improved communities and enhanced quality of living. The economic advantages of trails are profound: rail-trails catalyze small business growth, promote tourism, invigorate neighborhoods, reduce travel costs, and increase property values. They also improve the environment by reducing traffic congestion and pollution, preserving open space, conserving natural resources, and lowering air and water pollution levels. From a quality of life perspective, rail-trails are an invaluable means of providing safe transportation to work, school, and transit connections; opportunities to socialize with friends and family; and a means of recharging our bodies and spirits in the open air of the nation's countryside.

The power of trails to reconnect us has never been more essential than it is today, and the Rails-to-Trails Conservancy Midwest regional office commends each trail group listed in this guide for their work and dedication. They have helped advance the trail movement in the State of Ohio and improved the quality of life of each of its residents.

Using This Guide

The goal of this book is to educate people about trails and greenways in Ohio. Although every effort has been made to ensure the accuracy of information included here, trails and their conditions can change at any time, so please make use of the contact names, addresses, phone numbers, and email addresses when considering traveling to a particular trail. Each trail listing includes a map and information about endpoints, distance, surface type, status, permitted uses, and local contact for current trail information and conditions.

The state map on pages 2 and 3 shows the location of the individual trails throughout the state, along with their corresponding page number. In addition, an index, which lists each county and the trails therein, has been included on pages 4 and 5 and an alphabetical list of trails is on pages 6 and 7.

Business sponsors are listed in an alphabetical index beginning on page 8. Those located on or near a trail have also been noted on the individual trail maps. Please consider patronizing these sponsors when planning your trail experience to thank them for supporting the development of rail-trails in Ohio and the production of this guidebook.

Personal safety is the responsibility of each user. Trails can be busy recreational and alternate transportation corridors. Please heed the posted rules and regulations governing each trail and respect your fellow trail users. Helmets are the law in many areas for children and recommended for adults. However, a helmet cannot replace common sense. Have a safe and fun trail experience.

Every trail has a series of icons depicting uses allowed on the trail:

 Bicycling

 Running, Walking, Hiking

 Cross Country Skiing

 Snow Mobiling

 Horseback Riding

 Wheelchair Accessible

 In-Line Skating

Legend for Trail Maps:

 State Route

 Complete Trail

 Interstate Highway

 Proposed Trail

 U.S. Highway

 Major Highway

 City Limits

 Minor Highway

 Point of Interest

 Railroad Line

Waterways

 Parking

 Guide Sponsor

Membership Opportunities

About Rails-to-Trails Conservancy

Established in 1986, RTC is a national nonprofit public charity with more than 5,000 members in Ohio. The mission of RTC is to enhance America's countryside by converting thousands of miles of abandoned rail corridors and connecting open space into a nationwide network of public trails.

How to become an RTC member

Our efforts are wholly supported by the generous contributions of our members and friends – individuals and families like you. We invite you to join today by filling out the included membership form.

Membership/Gift Membership Levels:

Trailblazer Society	$1000
Advocate Membership	$ 500
Benefactor	$ 250
Business Membership	$ 100
Organization Membership	$ 50
Family Membership	$ 25
Individual Membership	$ 18

As a member of RTC, you will receive the following:

- A membership in the national and state organizations

- A subscription to our national magazine, Rails-to-Trails

- Discounts on books, merchandise and conferences

- Additional benefits for Trailblazer Society members

Membership Opportunities

You can help support the Rails-to-Trails Conservancy, a nonprofit charitable organization as qualified under Section 501(c)(3) of the Internal Revenue Code, by becoming a member.

To obtain a copy of RTC's current financial statement, annual report, and state registration, write to RTC at 1100 17th Street, NW, 10th Floor Washington, DC 20036, or call (202) 331-9696.

Sponsorship Opportunities

How to become a business sponsor

This guide is the product of dedicated trail builders and managers and would not be possible without the added support of local businesses in the communities where trails are open or planned/proposed.

If you would like to have your business noted on your local trail map and/or listed in the alphabetical services index, please return the Business Sponsorship Form by mail, or call the Ohio field office at (614) 837-6782.

Order Form

Publications

I want ___ copies of the Ohio Trails and Greenways guidebook. Price includes Ohio sales tax. Shipping is $3.50 for the first copy plus 50¢ for each additional copy. Trail groups, bike shops, bookstores and other volume sale outlets should contact the office for pricing and shipping.

Members	$14.41
Non-Members	$16.01
Subtotal	$_____

Memberships

My dues enroll me as a member of the Rails-to-Trails Conservancy, Ohio field office.

Trailblazer	$1000
Advocate	$ 500
Benefactor	$ 250
Business	$ 100
Family	$ 25
Individual	$ 18
Subtotal	$_____

Donations

❏ I want to assist the efforts in the State of Ohio. I am enclosing an additional gift to the Ohio field office.

Amount enclosed $_____

Please see previous page for more information on business sponsorship and advertising opportunities.

Total Enclosed $_____

Payment Type   ❑ Check
                        ❑ Visa
                        ❑ MasterCard
                        ❑ American Express
                        ❑ Discover Card

Credit card number

_____ - _____ - _____ - _____

Expiration date

_____

Signature

_____

Make checks payable to:

    RTC Ohio
    30 Liberty Street
    Canal Winchester, Ohio 43110

Name

_____

Address

_____

City

_____

State

_____

ZIP

_____

Phone

_____

(required for credit card orders)

Email

_____

Business Sponsor Form

Business Sponsor

○ I would like to have my business listed as a sponsor in the next edition of Ohio Trails and Greenways.

Contact name
_____

Title
_____

Business name
_____

Address
_____

City
_____

State
_____

ZIP
_____

Phone
_____

Fax
_____

Email
_____

Website
_____

Return to: RTC Ohio
          30 Liberty Street
          Canal Winchester, Ohio 43110

Call (614) 837-6782   Fax (614) 837-6783

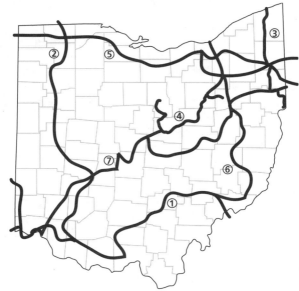

A trail system is composed of individual trails and trail segments. Currently, Ohio has seven trail systems that allow users to travel safe, scenic routes through rural, urban, and suburban areas. It is the goal of Rails-to-Trails Conservancy Ohio to play a critical role in the continued development of organized trail systems throughout the state, with connections to trails and trail systems in neighboring states and regions.

The Ohio Department of Natural Resources (ODNR) Ohio Trail Plan is a comprehensive inventory of both trails and trail systems in the State of Ohio. Rails-to-Trails Conservancy, in cooperation with ODNR, the Ohio Department of Transportation (ODOT), and trail groups throughout the State of Ohio, diligently works to support the growth and development of trails and trail systems in the Ohio Trail Plan.

1. American Discovery Trail
2. The Buckeye Trail
3. The Great Ohio Lake to River Greenway
4. The Heart of Ohio Trail
5. The North Coast Inland Trail
6. The North Country Scenic Trail
7. The Ohio to Erie Trail

American Discovery Trail

The American Discovery Trail (ADT) is a new breed of national trail – part city, part small town, part forest, part mountains, part desert – all in one trail. Its 6,300+ miles of continuous multi-use trail stretch from Cape Henlopen State Park, Delaware to Pt. Reyes National Seashore, California. It reaches across America, linking community to community in the first coast-to-coast non-motorized trail. The ADT provides trail users the opportunity to journey into the heart of all that is uniquely American – its culture, heritage, landscape and spirit.

The ADT incorporates trails designed for hiking, bicycle and equestrian use. Because it connects five national scenic trails and ten national historic trails, 23 national recreational trails, and many other local and regional trails, it is the backbone for a national trails system. It passes through metropolitan areas like San Francisco and Cincinnati, traces numerous pioneer trails, leads to 14 national parks and 16 national forests and visits more than 10,000 sites of historic, cultural and natural significance.

First Lady Hillary Rodham-Clinton honored the ADT as a National Millennium Trail in June 1999. More information about the ADT is available at www.discoverytrail.org.

The ADT route in Ohio is 521.5 miles long, on trails through public and private lands with landowner permission. The route uses the least-traveled public roads possible to connect off-road sections. The trail is marked with blue blazes for the Buckeye Trail section and ADT markers for connections to West Virginia and Indiana.

American Discovery
Trail Society
P. O. Box 20155
Washington, DC 20041
1-800-663-2387 or
703-753-0149
membership@discoverytrail.org
www.discoverytrail.org

The American Discovery Trail Route Through Ohio

1. Belpre to Chesterhill - 33.3 miles
2. Chesterhill (begin Buckeye Trail) to Sunday Creek Rd/SR78 - 16.1 miles
3. Sunday Creek Road/SR78 to Ohio SR664 - 55.9 miles
4. Ohio SR664 to SR 327 - 41.7 miles
5. Ohio SR327 to Pike Lake State Park -57.6 mi.
6. Pike Lake State Park to junction of Mineral Springs and Davis Memorial Road - 53 miles
7. Mineral Springs and Davis Memorial Roads to Long Lick and Sunshine Ridge Road - 41.8 miles
8. Sunshine Ridge Road to SR 774 and Grant Lake - 54.6 miles
9. Ohio SR 774 & Grant Lake to Eden Park, Cincinnati (leave Buckeye Trail) - 64.3 miles
10. Eden Park, Cincinnati to Elizabethtown - 33.6 miles
11. Elizabethtown to Richmond, Indiana (Northern route) - 69.6 miles

The Buckeye Trail

The Buckeye Trail is the only long-distance hiking trail located entirely in the state of Ohio, winding for 1,400 miles and reaching into every corner of the state. The trail follows old canal towpaths, abandoned railroad rights-of-way, rivers, lakeshores, rural byways, and footpaths over forested public and private lands. It passes through state and local parks, state and national forests, small towns, and urban areas, giving a unique perspective of the state.

First envisioned in the late 1950s as a trail from the Ohio River to Lake Erie, the Buckeye Trail evolved into a large loop, branching both north and east from Cincinnati. The separate legs rejoin in the Cuyahoga Valley National Recreation Area near Cleveland, and complete the trip to the lake.

The trail is identified by blue blazes, two inches wide by six inches high, on trees or poles. A single blaze marks the trail where the route is fairly straight or obvious, while a double blaze marks a turn with the upper blaze offset to indicate the new direction. A double blaze with no offset simply means pay attention because the trail route may not be obvious.

The trail is maintained and managed by the Buckeye Trail Association (BTA), a private, non-profit volunteer organization. First Lady Hillary-Rodham Clinton honored the Buckeye Trail as Ohio's Millennium Legacy Trail in a ceremony in Washington on October 21, 1999. Only one trail per state is so honored. More information about The Buckeye Trail is available at www.buckeyetrail.org.

For further information on trail status contact:

Herb Hulls
Buckeye Trail Association
P. O. Box 254
Worthington, OH 43085
(740) 585-2603
info@buckeyetrail.org
www.buckeyetrail.org

Jack Watkins
(614) 451-4233
1-800-881-3062

Great Ohio Lake to River Greenway

This trail system will be a 100+-mile-long green band of protected open space running through farmlands and woodlands, over hills, and along beautiful waterways. This greenway, built on unused railroad lines and adjacent corridors, will connect Lake Erie at Ashtabula Harbor with the Ohio River at East Liverpool. When complete, the Great Ohio Lake to River Greenway will provide transportation and recreational benefits for Northeast Ohioans.

The Great Ohio Lake to River Greenway will provide a multi-use recreational and alternate transportation corridor where children and adults can walk, run, cycle, cross-country ski, or, in some areas, ride horseback. The greenway preserves wildlife habitats and generates economic benefits for the community by increasing the number of visitors to the area. It also connects communities that once were linked by rail service.

By preserving and protecting the former railroad corridor, greenway developers have made it possible to maintain the integrity of the route for future infrastructure use.

Additional information about individual segments of the greenway are available in Ashtabula, Columbiana, Mahoning, and Trumbull County trail listings.

For further information on trail status contact:

Ashtabula Co. Parks
Charlie Kohli
25 W. Jefferson St.
Jefferson, OH 44047
(440) 576-0717

Friends of the
Western Reserve Greenway
Ada Callahan-Sutter
Phone: (330) 856-6750
adaz@onecom.com

Mahoning County
Susan Dicken
P. O. Box 596
Canfield, OH 44406
(330) 702-3000

Columbiana Co. Park
Dave Goerig
130 W. Maple Street
Lisbon, OH 44432
(330) 424-9078

Western Reserve Greenway
Kevin Grippi, Trail Coordinator
25 West Jefferson Street
Jefferson, Ohio 44047
(440) 964-3882
grippi@ashtabula.kent.edu
www.ashtabulacountymetroparks.org

Heart of Ohio Trail

Local trail groups and Rails-to-Trails Conservancy share a vision of a completed rail-trail system linking Richland, Knox, Holmes, Wayne and Stark counties from Mansfield to Massillon. Locally, the vision focuses on specific stretches of trails linking homes, schools and parks. Regionally, the vision extends to include trails linking counties and landscapes. Nationally, the vision expands to include a system of trails connecting coast to coast and border to border.

The system will connect Dalton, Butler, Fredericksburg, Mt. Vernon and Danville into a regional and national network of trails. Visitors to Richland County will experience the Gorman Nature Center and North Lake Park. Knox County offers the charm of Gambier, breathtaking scenery, and "The Bridge of Dreams" over the Mohican River. Wayne County can share its variety of land-scapes and Amish communities and Stark County its portion of the Ohio and Erie Canal National Heritage Canalway and the link to the Ohio to Erie Trail. Holmes County offers Baddow Pass, Killbuck Marsh and a shared corridor with Amish buggies.

The dedication of the local trail groups has resulted in many completed portions of the Heart of Ohio Trail System, and other portions are in various stages of planning and development. The Richland B&O Trail stretches 18.4 miles from Mansfield to Butler. The Kokosing Gap Trail runs 14 miles from Mt. Vernon to Danville. The Mohican Valley trail is 4.8 miles from Danville to Brinkhaven and features the "Bridge of Dreams," Ohio's second longest covered bridge, spanning 370 feet over the Mohican River. The Sippo Valley Trail runs 10.5 miles from Dalton to Massillon. The Holmes County Trail from Brinkhaven to Glenmont and Killbuck to Fredericktown is partially accessible on mixed surfaces. Work continues toward completion.

For further information on trail status contact:

Holmes County
Joan Simcack
Holmes County Trail
P. O. Box 95
Millersburg, OH 44654
330-279-2643
holmestrail@earthlink.net
www.holmestrail.org

Knox County
Phil Samuell
Kokosing Gap Trail
P. O. Box 129
Gambier, OH 43022
740-397-0311 ext. 432
www.kokosinggaptrail.org

Mohican Valley Trail Board
P. O. Box 261
Howard, OH 43028
740-599-6720

Richland County
Steve McKee
Richland Co.
Park District
2295 Lexington Ave.
Mansfield, OH 44907
419-884-3764

Wayne County
Keith Workman
Rails-to-Trails
of Wayne County
2786 Chippewa Road
Orrville, OH 44667
330-682-7188
kcw2786@copper.net

The North Coast Inland Trail

The North Coast Inland Trail, NCIT, is a partially open 65-mile trail that will link with other northern Ohio trails to connect Pennsylvania with Michigan and Indiana across northern Ohio. The NCIT travels through Lorain, Huron, Sandusky, and Wood Counties along the former Toledo, Norwalk, and Cleveland Railroad. Trail surfaces are different along the various completed segments.

In Lorain County, trail users may travel 14 miles on asphalt between Elyria and Kipton, passing through historic Oberlin, home of Oberlin College. In Huron County, between Peru Center Road and North West Street, there is a 3.6-mile gravel trail segment that is available for use but will open officially in early 2005. This segment of the trail has two particularly beautiful areas where it crosses the east and west branches of the Huron River. From Clyde to Fremont in Sandusky County, the asphalt trail segment has been open as a rail-with-trail since 1997. The trail is separated from the active rail line by water and trees, crosses Green Creek, and ends near the Biggs-Ketner Park in Fremont. The 2.7-mile crushed limestone trail segment in Elmore, Ottawa County, takes the trail user across the Portage River and Sugar Creek and links downtown Elmore with schools, homes, and green spaces. In Wood County, the 1.9-mile asphalt trail segment is the first phase of what will be a 12-mile link between the NCIT and the Wabash Cannonball Trail (page 92). Currently, this segment connects Lake Township Park and the downtown area of the Village of Walbridge.

Parking and trail access are available in the communities where trail segments are complete. In Lorain County, Kipton visitors may find parking in Kipton Park south along Baird Road off of State Route 113. Take State Route 113 into Elyria, turn south on Lorain Boulevard to Gateway Boulevard and then west on Third Street to the north terminus of the trail. Additional parking may be found on the street in Oberlin at State Route 58 in the downtown area. Trail visitors to Huron County will want to exit US Route 20 in Monroeville, turning south to Peru Center Road. Some parking is available in Norwalk at North West Street on the west side of the city.

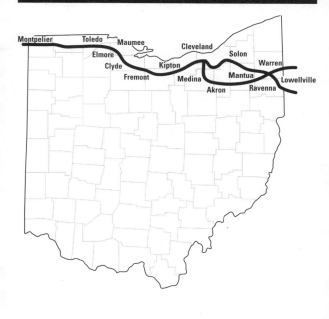

For further information on trail status contact:

Dan Martin
Lorain County Metro Parks
12882 Diagonal Road
LaGrange, OH 44050
440-458-5121
bvoit@loraincountyparks.com
www.loraincountymetroparks.com

The North Country Scenic Trail

The North Country Scenic Trail was first conceived in the 1970s, but the real birth of this trail dates from March 5, 1980, when the North Country Trail was included in a package of amendments to the National Parks and Recreation Act of 1978 and signed into law on that date by President Carter. The act authorized a total of eight national scenic trails. This trail is modeled after its cousin, the Appalachian Trail, and is the longest National Scenic Trail in the country. The goal of the trail is 4,600 miles across seven states: North Dakota, Minnesota, Wisconsin, Michigan, Ohio, Pennsylvania, and New York. Much of the trail is still in the proposed stages.

The National Park Service adopted the Comprehensive Plan for the North Country National Scenic Trail in September 1982. The comprehensive plan, as it was adopted, gave several key directions to the trail. Most importantly, it gave the trail direction as a "non-motorized multiple use trail," specifically authorized to allow non-motorized use other than hiking if approved by local managing authority.

The North Country Trail Association -- a grassroots nonprofit organization striving to build, maintain, protect and promote the North Country National Scenic Trail -- oversees the trail. Volunteers throughout the seven states perform nearly all of the work being completed on the trail. These volunteers are organized into local chapters.

First Lady Hillary Rodham-Clinton honored the North Country Scenic Trail as a National Millennium Trail in June 1999.

For further information on trail status contact:

North Country Trail Association
229 East Main Street
Lowell, MI 49331
Phone: 616-897-5987 X3103
FAX: 616-897-6605
robcorbett@northcountrytrail.org

Ohio to Erie Trail

Begun in 1991, the Ohio to Erie Trail (OET) is the backbone of an inter-connecting system of trails from the Ohio River to Lake Erie. It not only links Ohio's three main urban centers - Cincinnati, Columbus and Cleveland - but also connects a large number of Ohio's towns and villages through trail networks along the primary route. The Ohio to Erie Trail begins in downtown Cincinnati and goes north along the Little Miami Scenic Trail to the Xenia hub. From Xenia, it heads northeast to London, follows the Big Darby Creek to Plain City, and then heads into Columbus through Hilliard.

North of Columbus, the OET diverges into two routes: the Heart of Ohio Trail through Mt. Vernon and Millersburg, and the Panhandle through Newark, Coshocton, and New Philadelphia.

The northern section of the OET follows the Ohio & Erie National Heritage Canalway to downtown Cleveland. The OET is over 400 miles long and nearly two-thirds complete. Hikers, bikers, bird watchers, horseback riders, cross-country skiers, and wheel-chair users enjoy this trail as it passes through quiet woods, lush fields, rural villages, and urban centers.

The nonprofit Ohio to Erie Trail Fund raises funds to buy land for the trail and deeds the land to local political subdivisions to build and maintain it. Thanks to gifts from individuals, businesses, bike clubs and foundations, the Ohio to Erie Trail Fund has purchased many miles of former railroad right-of-way for the trail since the fund was established in 1991.

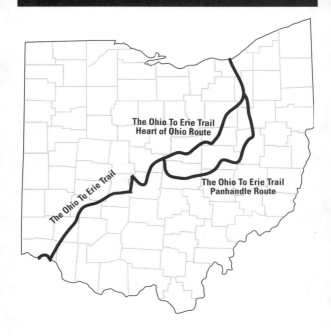

For further information on trail status contact:

Jerry Rampelt
Executive Director
Ohio to Erie Trail Fund
P. O. Box 21246
Columbus, OH 43221
614-284-2178
webmaster@ohiotoerietrail.org
www.ohiotoerietrail.org

Miami Erie Canal

Allen, Auglaize, Miami, Shelby, Van Wert

State of Project: Open
End Points: Delphos (N), Piqua (S) and Sidney (SE)
Length: 59 miles
Surface: Grass, dirt, and compacted stone

The Miami Erie Canal was built between 1825 and 1845 as an engineering marvel stretching from Cincinnati to Toledo. This canal was heavily used until competition from the railroad caused the decline of the canal system. This canal was last used commercially in 1929. After the decline of the canal, the towpath was utilized for the interurban line that served west Auglaize and Shelby Counties.

The Miami Erie Canal passes through many quaint towns and villages. Numerous locks, spillways and historic buildings remain from the canal era. Much of the local history has been preserved in the many museums that are located along the corridor. The trail connects three state parks, local parks, community trails, and historic sites. This trail is a segment of the Buckeye Trail (page 24) and North Country Scenic Trail (page 32).

Horses are allowed along the trail from Delphos to Spencerville. Only small sections of trail are appropriate for street bikes.

Portions of the trail from Lockington to Sidney are not complete. Contact Miami Erie Canal Corridor Association for current information.

Parking and access are available along the corridor in Delphos, Spencerville, St. Mary's, New Bremen, Minister, Fort Loramie, and Sidney. Additional staging areas may be found along State Route 66.

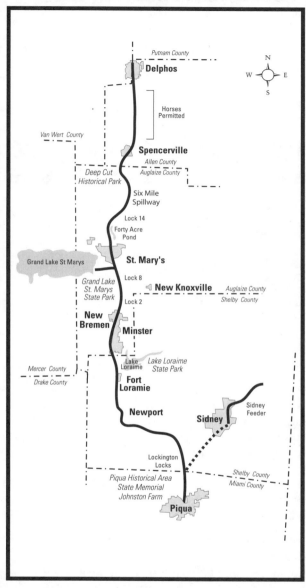

Contact and Tourist Information:

L. Neal Brady, Director
Miami Erie Canal Corridor Association
P. O. Box 722
St. Mary's, OH 45869
419-733-6451
meccadirector@bright.net

Western Reserve Greenway

Ashtabula, Trumbull

State of Project: Open
End Points: West 52nd Street and county line (N) and County line to Champion Street (S)
Length: 43 miles
Surface: Asphalt

The Western Reserve Greenway lies within Ohio's two northeastern counties and is a part of the Great Ohio Lake to River Greenway (page 26). This 100-mile trail will connect Lake Erie with the Ohio River through Ashtabula, Columbiana, Mahoning, and Trumbull Counties. The former Pennsylvania Railroad corridor roughly parallels State Route 45 to the east, intersects five state routes, and passes under Interstate 90.

Trail users will find scenic waterways and bridges between quaint rural villages, fertile farmland and protected wetlands as they travel along the greenway. Wildlife seen along the corridor includes eagles, blue herons, ducks, and turkeys. The north terminus of the trail is located at what was once the last Ohio stop of the Underground Railroad. Plans for the trail include developing interpretive signs that explain the Underground Railroad and the role of Ashtabula County.

Trail users with snowmobiles should be aware that snowmobiles are allowed only along the Ashtabula County segment of the trail and that no studs are allowed to be used while on the trail.

Parking and trail access are available at Woodman Avenue in the City of Ashtabula, Old Austinburg Road, State Route 307, and Lampson Road in Ashtabula County. In Trumbull County, parking is available at Hyde-Oakfield Road, State Route 305, and Educational Highway.

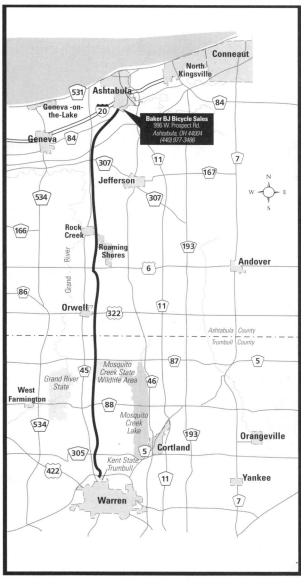

Contact and Tourist Information:

Kevin Grippi
Volunteer Trail Coordinator
Ashtabula County Metroparks
25 West Jefferson Street
Jefferson, OH 44047
440-964-3882
grippi@ashtabula.kent.edu
www.ashtabulacountymetroparks.org

Ada Callahan-Sutter
Co-Chair, Trumbull County
Friends of the Western Reserve
Greenway
330-856-6750
adaz@onecom.com
www.greenway.co.trumbull.oh.us

Hockhocking Adena Bikeway

Athens

State of Project: Open
End Points: Nelsonville (N) and Athens (S)
Length: 19.4 miles
Surface: Asphalt

The Hockhocking Adena Bikeway is named in honor of the first inhabitants of the area. "Hocking," which means "bottleneck" or "twisted," was the native American name for the Hocking River. "Adena" reflects the history of the Adena Indians who lived in the Hocking Valley over 2,000 years ago.

From 1829 to 1842, this corridor was used as a towpath that carried goods to Carroll where it joined the Ohio and Erie Canal. In 1870, the Columbus and Hocking Operating Valley Railroad began operating on this corridor and served the area until the late 1800s when a flood severely damaged the railroad.

Now the Hockhocking Adena Bikeway follows the same beautiful corridor along the Hocking River, linking Hocking College with Ohio University and beyond.

Parking and trail access are available at East State Street in Athens, Beaumont/Selma off of State Route 682 in Wayne National Forest, and at Robbins Cabin on the grounds of Hocking College.

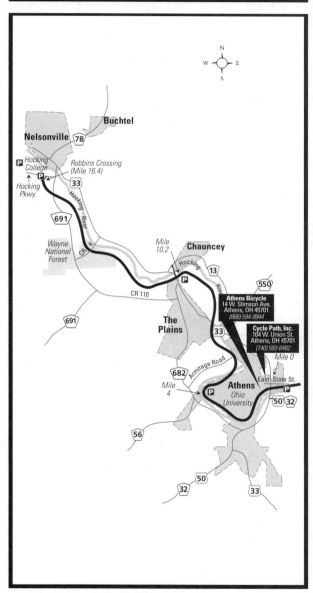

Contact and Tourist Information:

Linda Hart, Director
Hockhocking Adena Bikeway
Advisory Committee
667 East State Street
Athens, OH 45701
1-800-878-9767
lhart@athensohio.com
www.athensohio.com

Moonville Rail Trail

Athens, Vinton

State of Project: Partially open
End Points: Mineral (E) and Red
Diamond Plant (W)
Length: 16 miles
Surface: Ballast

The Moonville Rail Trail is a 16-mile trail that utilizes the former Marietta and Cincinnati Railroad that began service in the 1850s. This railroad provided only industrial service, never carrying passengers because of its proximity to the Red Diamond Dynamite plant.

This new rail-trail will take visitors through beautiful southeast Ohio forest lands including Zaleski State Forest; the communities of Zaleski and Mineral; past New Marshfield School, which ceased operation in 2004, after more than 100 years of continuous use, and Lake Hope wetland areas. The corridor holds water on both sides of the trail creating a wetland area that is home to numerous species of flora and fauna. Additional points of interest along this trail are two unique and historic tunnels. King Switch Tunnel is a 120-foot structure carved through the rock and lined by a series of 12x12 wooden beams. The Moonville Tunnel is brick lined and thought by some to be haunted.

Currently, 10 miles of ballast surfaced trail, perfect for horses or walkers and hikers, are available from Lake Hope School to the Moonville Tunnel. Future plans are for the trail to extend approximately eight miles to the east and link with the Hockhocking Adena Bikeway (page 40) in Athens. To the west the trail will eventually extend to the Jackson County line.

To reach parking and trail access at Lake Hope School take State Route 278 to Lake Hope Dam. Turn east on to Wheelabout Road and continue approximately half a mile to the school.

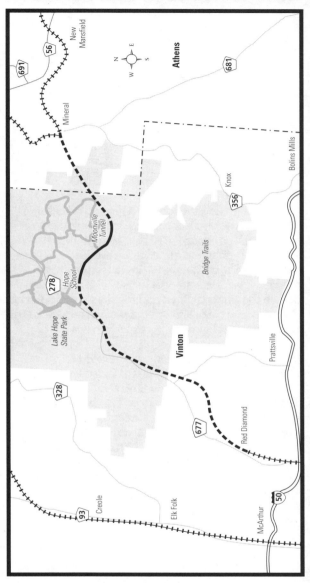

Contact and Tourist Information:

Neil Shaw, President
Moonville Rail-Trail Association
938 Roley Road
Logan, OH 43138
740-385-5306
Nb_lazyvalleyfarms@hotmail.com
www.moonvillerailtrail.org

Belmont

State of Project: Partially open
End Points: Ballfield Road (N)
and Reservoir Road (S)
Length: 7 miles
Surface: Asphalt

This bikeway along the former Wheeling & Lake Erie railroad has the distinction of including Ohio's first rail-trail tunnel. The tunnel is 522 feet long and 42 feet high with special lighting to enhance its cave-like feel. The north headwall of the tunnel has been rebuilt and includes a staircase leading to a two-level plaza overlook on the National Road and the city's historic district. The top of the plaza also offers a wonderful view of the bikeway 82 feet below.

Another feature of this trail is the elevated former rail trestle, 342 feet long and 62 feet above the valley floor. The rugged hills of eastern Ohio and an adjoining "Mail Pouch Barn" provide a scenic backdrop to the rehabilitated bridge. A beautiful centerpiece of this project is a 31-foot diameter gazebo situated in the middle of a traffic circle for use by bicyclists and pedestrians. The gazebo is located in the flower gardens of Hub Park, which includes a nature walk and a gently flowing stream.

Parking is available at both ends of the trail. To reach the south terminus take exit 216 off of Interstate 70, continue south on Route 9 for eight-tenths of a mile to Reservoir Road (Township Road 278). To reach the north terminus, at the four-way stop behind the courthouse in St. Clairsville, turn onto North Market Street and continue for nine-tenths of a mile to the Bikeway Crossing, turn right onto Ballfield Road.

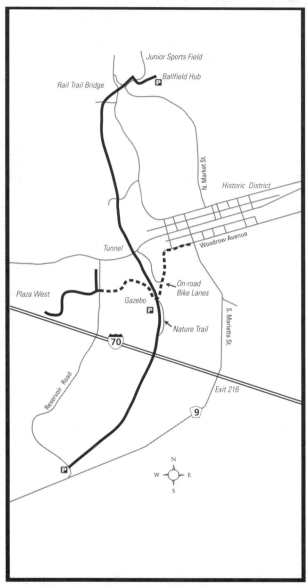

Contact and Tourist Information:

Dennis Bigler
Director of Public Services,
City of St. Clairsville
P. O. Box 537
100 North Market Street
St. Clairsville OH 43950
740-695-0156
dops@1st.net
www.stclairsville.com

Butler, Montgomery, Warren

State of Project: Partially open
End Points: Island MetroPark (N)
and Hamilton (S)
Length: 63.1 miles
Surface: Asphalt

This trail begins at Island MetroPark on Helena Street. Trail users may follow either the east or west side of the riverbank south along the Great Miami River to Stewart Street. At Stewart Street, the west side trail turns east across the bridge and ends at the intersection with the east bank trail. Trail users may utilize the Rubicon Trail east on Stewart Street to the University of Dayton.

The trail continues south along the east side of the river past Carillon Park, passing through the cities of Moraine, West Carrollton, and Miamisburg before ending at Crains Run Park just north of the Warren and Montgomery County line. A 3.7-mile segment of trail is expected to be completed in 2005 from Crains Run Park to Baxter Drive.

Trail users may follow State Route 73 south from Baxter Drive to the State Route 4 bridge over the Great Miami River to re-connect with the 2.6-mile trail that follows the Great Miami River south through Middletown terminating at Bicentennial Commons Park.

Plans are for the trail to continue from Bicentennial Commons Park four miles to Miami Erie Canal Excello Lock Park and then continue the route ten miles south. Five miles of trail from Rentschler Forest Preserve to the Main High Bridge in downtown Hamilton will be constructed in 2005.

Currently, from Main High Bridge trail users may travel 4.3 miles south along the east bank of the Great Miami River to the city of Fairfield. The trail ends at Waterworks Park.

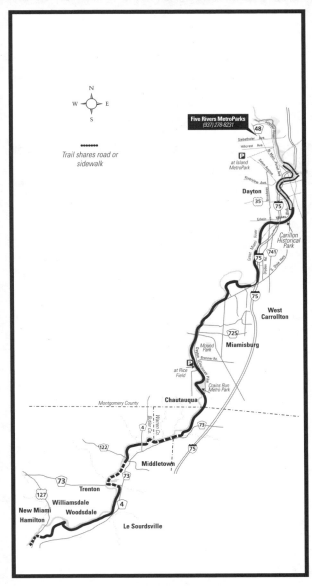

Trail shares road or
sidewalk

Five Rivers MetroParks
(937) 278-8231

Contact and Tourist Information:

Hans Landefeld
Miami Conservancy District
38 East Monument Avenue
Dayton, OH 45402
937-223-1278 X 3223
hlandefeld@miamiconservancy.org
www.miamiconservancy.org

Craig Wenner
Operations Manager
Five Rivers MetroParks
1375 East Siebenthaler Avenue
Dayton, OH 45414
937-278-8231
cwenner@metroparks.org
www.metroparks.org

Champaign

State of Project: Open
End Points: Community Drive (N)
and County Line Road (S)
Length: 12 miles
Surface: Asphalt

The Simon Kenton Trail connects the city of Urbana and Champaign County with a developing network of statewide multi-use trails. Trail users may begin on the east side of Urbana at Community Drive, curve through town along the former Erie-Lackawana Railroad and a part of the former Pennsylvania Railroad, and head southwest into the county, past Urbana University (home of the Johnny Appleseed Museum), to Cedar Bog, and end at County Line Road at the Champaign and Clark County line. It is possible to continue into Clark County and link up with the Little Miami Scenic Trail (page 54), the Greene County Trail System, and the Ohio to Erie Trail.

Parking and trail access are available at the east terminus of the trail in the city of Urbana at Community Drive and US Route 36 and at Melvin Miller Park at Childrens Home Road. Urbana Station, located at 644 Miami Street, also offers some parking. In the county, parking may be found at State Route 55, two-and-a-half miles south at Woodburn Road east of US Route 68, and at the southern trail terminus at County Line Road.

In the future, trail developers would like to create a crossing from US Route 36 to State Route 29 so that trail users will be able to reach the County Library.

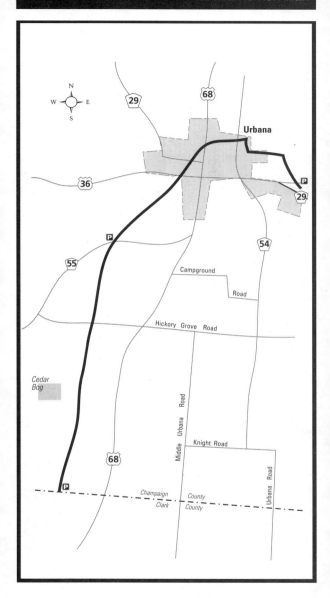

Contact and Tourist Information:

Nancy Lokai-Baldwin, President
Simon Kenton Pathfinders
P. O. Box 91
Urbana, OH 43078
937-484-3335
nlb@foryou.net
www.simonkentontrail.org

Buck Creek Trail

Clark

State of Project: Open
End Points: Buck Creek State Park (Croft Rd) (E) and Limestone St (W)
Length: 3.1 miles
Surface: Asphalt

Buck Creek Trail (BCT) was developed by the City of Springfield to provide a scenic view of Buck Creek and its adjoining wooded areas. Along the BCT the user travels through Snyder, Veterans, and Old Reid Parks. The BCT also connects to the Clark County segment of the Simon Kenton Trail (page 52), next to the Carleton Davidson Memorial Stadium at about mid-trail. From the trail head at Pumphouse Road, trail users are able to travel the trail north through Old Reid Park across Croft Road into Buck Creek State Park.

Parking and trail access are available at the trail head at 1230 Pumphouse Road, where it comes to a "T" at Columbus Road in Springfield. There are temporary restroom facilities at this trailhead, but no water.

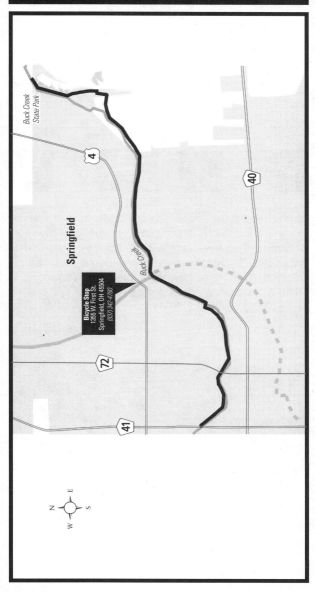

Contact and Tourist Information:

Jim Campbell
Open Space Manager
National Trail Parks and Rec. District
1301 Mitchell Blvd.
Springfield, OH 45503
937-328-PARK (7275)
jcampbell@ci.springfield.oh.us
www.nationaltrailparksandrec.org

Tim Smith, CEO
National Trail Parks and Rec. District
1301 Mitchell Blvd.
Springfield, OH 45503
937-328-PARK (7275)
tsmith@ci.springfield.oh.us
www.nationaltrailparksandrec.org

Clark County Simon Kenton Trail

Clark

State of Project: Open
End Points: County Line Rd. (N) and Jefferson St. at Little Miami Scenic Trail North Terminus (S)
Length: 8.5 miles
Surface: Asphalt

This 8.5-mile trail connects Springfield in Clark County and Urbana in Champaign County, providing the trail user with 16 miles of beautiful vistas of rich Ohio farmland and other natural settings. This trail connects from Urbana to the Little Miami Scenic Trail (page 54) at Jefferson Street in Springfield.

Trail access and parking are available at the trailhead located at 75 Villa Road. To reach the trailhead on Villa Road take State Route 72, turn east at Villa Road, and follow it around to the trailhead. Additional parking is available at 500 Eagle City Road, east of US Route 68 in Springfield.

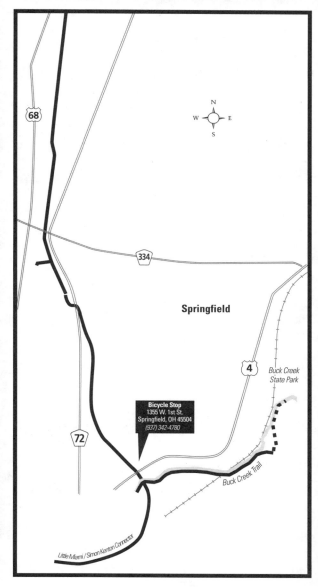

Contact and Tourist Information:

Jim Campbell
Open Space Manager
National Trail Parks
and Recreation District
1301 Mitchell Blvd.
Springfield, OH 45503
937-328-PARK (7275)
jcampbell@ci.springfield.oh.us
www.nationaltrailparksandrec.org

Tim Smith, CEO
National Trail Parks
and Recreation District
1301 Mitchell Blvd.
Springfield, OH 45503
937-328-PARK (7275)
tsmith@ci.springfield.oh.us
www.nationaltrailparksandrec.org

Little Miami Scenic Trail

Clark, Clermont, Greene, Hamilton, Warren

State of Project: Open
End Points: Springfield (N)
and Milford (S)
Length: 70 miles
Surface: Asphalt

The Little Miami Scenic Trail (LMST) uses the former Little Miami Railroad Company corridor that once connected Cincinnati with Sandusky. The town of Xenia became a hub for the railroad. In 1966, the last train rolled through Xenia and now the rebuilt depot serves as a hub for the trails.

The LMST starts in Milford with parking available at the trailhead at US Route 50 and State Route 126. The trail continues for 70 miles to Springfield, meandering through five counties of rolling farm country, tall cliffs, steep gorges, and forests.

Birdwatchers enjoy the abundance and variety of colorful songbirds in the park, while the trail's shaded slopes offer more than 340 species of wildflowers.

A 128-foot bridge over the Little Miami River and a 126-foot, seven-inch bridge over Massie Creek along the railroad corridor were restored for trail use.

Parking lots, restrooms, public phones, and trail access points are available in Loveland, Morrow, Corwin, Xenia, Yellow Springs, and Springfield, with restored train depots located along the trail in Xenia and Yellow Springs.

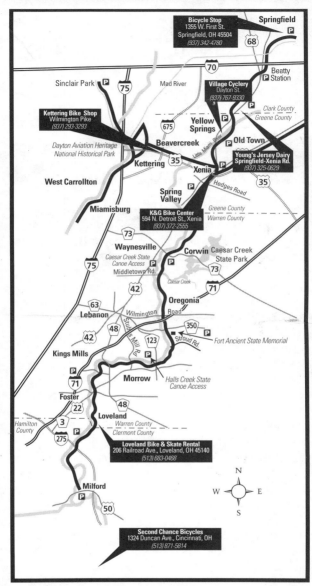

Bicycle Stop
1355 W. First St.
Springfield, OH 45504
(937) 342-4780

Springfield

68

70

Sinclair Park

75

Mad River

Beatty Station

Village Cyclery
Dayton St.
(937) 767-9330

Kettering Bike Shop
Wilmington Pike
(937) 293-3293

Clark County
Greene County

Yellow Springs

675

Beavercreek

Little Miami River

Old Town

*Dayton Aviation Heritage
National Historical Park*

Kettering

35

Xenia

Young's Jersey Dairy
Springfield-Xenia Rd.
(937) 325-0629

West Carrollton

Hedges Road

35

Spring Valley

K&G Bike Center
594 N. Detroit St., Xenia
(937) 372-2555

Greene County
Warren County

Miamisburg

73

Waynesville

*Caesar Creek State
Canoe Access*
Middletown Rd.

Corwin

**Caesar Creek
State Park**

75

42

Caesar Creek

73

71

63

Oregonia

Lebanon

Wilmington Road

42

48

350

123

Stroud Rd.

Fort Ancient State Memorial

Kings Mills

Stubbs Mill Rd.

71

Morrow

*Halls Creek State
Canoe Access*

Foster

22

48

3

Loveland

Warren County
Clermont County

275

Loveland Bike & Skate Rental
206 Railroad Ave., Loveland, OH 45140
(513) 683-0468

Hamilton County

N
W — E
S

Milford

50

Second Chance Bicycles
1324 Duncan Ave., Cincinnati, OH
(513) 871-5814

Contact and Tourist Information:

Greene County Section
Jim Schneider, Trail Manager
Greene County Parks and Rec.
651 Dayton - Xenia Road
Xenia, OH 45385
937-562-7440
jschneider@co.greene.oh.us

Jim Campbell
National Trails and Parks
and Recreation District
76 East High Street
Springfield, OH 45502
937-328-7275
jcampbell@ci.springfield.oh.us
www.nationaltrailsparksandrec.com

Caesar Creek State Park
8570 East State Route 73
Waynesville, OH 45068
513-897-3055

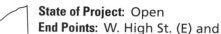

Prairie Grass Trail (Ohio to Erie Trail)

Clark, Madison

State of Project: Open
End Points: W. High St. (E) and
Massie Creek Rd. (W)
Length: 22.5 miles
Surface: Asphalt

Until the 1990s the railroad corridor that this trail utilizes was an active rail bed, and the surrounding prairie land continued to be protected by railroad practices that preserved the immediate area in its natural state. The trail managing organization is committed to the continued protection of this land and has instituted a vigorous conservation program that includes a prohibition on mowing. Trail users enjoy the many species of prairie wildlife that have returned to the area. Species of prairie flowers that have been seen along the trail include grey-headed coneflower, butterfly milkweed, sartwell's sedge, wild petunia, flowering spruge, and royal catchfly.

The newest segment of the Prairie Grass Trail takes the trail user into the City of London's historic downtown district. Among the many interesting buildings is the Historic London Train Depot, where President Lincoln stopped in February 1861 to give a speech on his way to take office in Washington, DC.

Parking and trail access are available at the trail-head in Cedarville; the train depot in South Charleston at 147 West Mound Street; and behind the Madison County Senior Center at 280 West High Street in London, along US Route 42 south of Midway Street near the south end of the city. Water is also available at the train depot and the Senior Center.

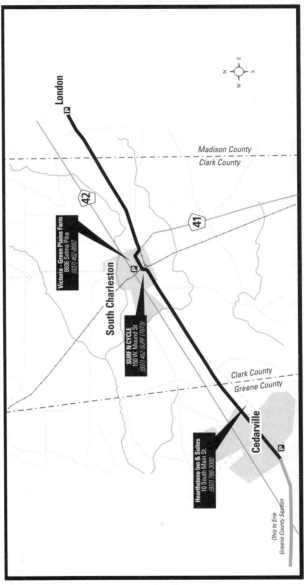

Contact and Tourist Information:

Jim Campbell
Open Space Manager
National Trail Parks
and Recreation District
1301 Mitchell Blvd.
Springfield, OH 45503
937-328-PARK (7275)
jcampbell@ci.springfield.oh.us
www.nationaltrailparksandrec.org

Friends of Madison County
Parks and Trails
P. O. Box 308
London, OH 43140
740-852-7833
fmcpt@columbus.rr.com
www.fmcpt.com

4-C Bicentennial Trail

Clinton

State of Project: Partially open
End Points: Southeast
Neighborhood Park (E)
and David Williams Park (W)
Length: 4 miles
Surface: Asphalt and natural

Plans are under way to connect the 4-C to a connector trail between David Williams and Denver Williams Parks. The connector then will join the Lowe's Drive path completed in 2003, along the east side of Wilmington.

Plans are also underway to connect the 4-C to the Luther Warren Peace Path that travels to the west end of the city.

Eventually, trail users will be able to travel east and west on approximately four miles of trail around and through the city of Wilmington. Trail planners anticipate having the new section of trail available December 2004.

Parking is available in David Williams Park, Denver Williams Park, and Southeast Neighborhood Park.

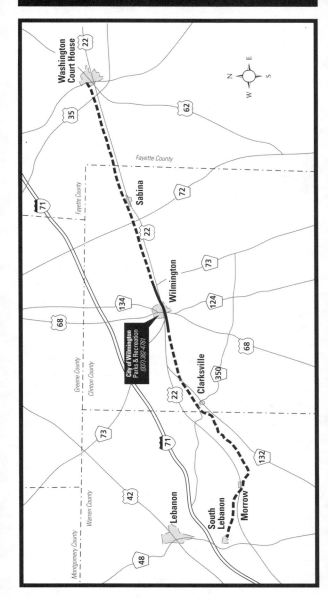

Contact and Tourist Information:

Lori Williams, Chair
Clinton Rails-to-Trails Coalition
116 Todds Ridge Road
Wilmington, OH 45177
937-382-3682
crtc@cinci.rr.com
www.clintonrailtrails.com

Scott Parrish, Superintendent
City of Wilmington Parks
& Recreation Department
69 North South Street
Wilmington, OH 45177
937-382-4781
sparrish@ci.wilmington.oh.us
www.ci.wilmington.oh.us

Little Beaver Creek Greenway Trail

Columbiana

State of Project: Open
End Points: Leetonia (N)
and Lisbon (S)
Length: 12 miles
Surface: Asphalt and Gravel

This trail runs parallel to the Middle Fork of the Little Beaver Creek and has many beautiful and interesting features including glacial outwashes, upland fields, mature ravine woodlots, and wetland wildlife habitats. Remnants of the industrial past also dot the trail with the remains of lime kilns, pig iron furnaces, coal mines, and coke ovens. The trail features a covered bridge and a connection to the Sandy Beaver Canal Towpath.

As a segment of the Great Ohio Lake to River Greenway (page 26), the Little Beaver Creek Greenway is a part of the trail system that begins in Ashtabula County and continues through Trumbull, Mahoning, and into Columbiana Counties. When complete, the Great Ohio Lake to River Greenway will be over 100 miles long.

Visitors to the Little Beaver Creek Greenway Trail may find parking and trail access from State Route 11. Exit on to State Route 154, heading west toward Lisbon. In Lisbon, State Route 154 becomes State Route 30 West. Continue along State Route 30 to State Route 164, and head south at the court house. Continue approximately a quarter-mile. Watch for trail signs. Parking will be on the right. To the north terminus of the trail, take old State Route 344 to State Route 558 to the trail entrance and parking area. Additional parking and access are available about mid-trail in Salem at Eagleton Road. Take State Route 45 south to Teegarden Road (County Road 41 West) to the covered bridge. Parking and trail entrance are by the bridge.

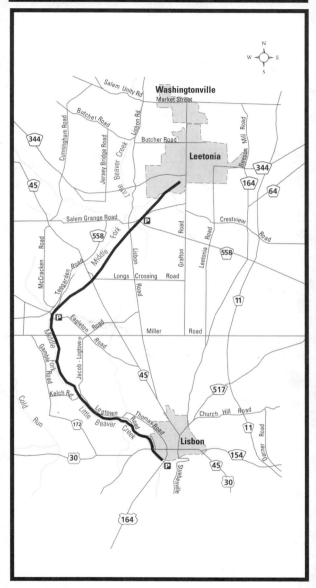

Contact and Tourist Information:

Dave Goerig
Columbiana County Parks
130 West Maple Street
Lisbon, OH 44432
330-424-9078
ccdod@sbcglobal.net
www.bicycletrail.com

Coshocton Three Rivers Bikeway

Coshocton

State of Project: Open
End Points: Lake Park (N), Roscoe Village (SW), and Sycamore St. (S)
Length: 3.5 miles
Surface: Asphalt

The Coshocton Three Rivers Bikeway provides safe and direct access from the City of Coshocton to the Lake Park Recreational Complex and historic Roscoe Village. Trail users cross under US Route 36, thereby eliminating the need to cross five lanes of busy traffic. The trail connects to an already existing trail in the Lake Park Complex.

Eventually, the Coshocton Trail will add another 23.1 miles as part of the Ohio to Erie Trail (page 34), that will connect Cincinnati with Cleveland through Columbus. When complete, this phase will link Coshocton with Dresden to the southwest, and Newcomerstown to the east.

Trail access is available all along the trail. Visitors to the area might prefer to park at Lake Park which is accessible via State Route 83 north. Turn west at the sign for Lake Park Complex. Restrooms and water fountains are available at the Lake Park Complex parking area.

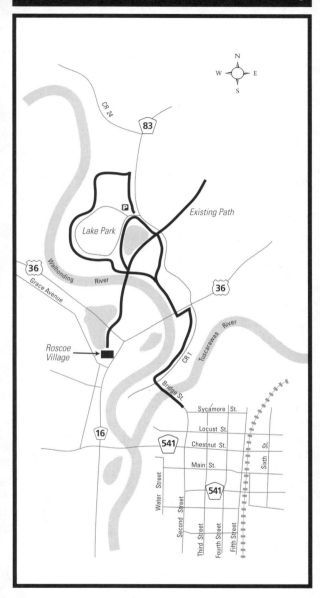

Contact and Tourist Information:

Steve Miller, Director
Coshocton Park District
23253 State Route 83
Coshocton, OH 43812
740-622-7528
steve_miller@coshoctonlakepark.com

Cleveland Lakefront Bikeway

Cuyahoga

State of Project: Partially open
End Points: Euclid Beach Park (E) and Ninth Street (W)
Length: 10.1 miles
Surface: Asphalt

The Cleveland Lakefront Bikeway follows the Lake Erie shoreline from East Ninth Street west to Euclid Beach Park. Almost totally flat, this trail is a combination of paved pathway, signed on-road bike route, and widened sidewalks.

The trail begins at the Rock and Roll Hall of Fame and Great Lakes Science Museum at East Ninth Street near downtown Cleveland and the Rapid Transit line. Heading east, trail users pass the Burke Lakefront Airport and Gordon Park, where the trail links with the Harrison Dillard Bikeway (page 68), and offers the trail user an additional link with Rockefeller Park and University Circle district. Continuing east on the Lakefront Bikeway, one travels along a quiet, two-lane street through the suburb of Bratenahl and its turn-of-the-century mansions. Beyond Bratenahl the route moves onto a busier four-lane signed bike route along Lakeshore Boulevard all the way to historic Euclid Beach Park. There is an additional mile of path that takes the user to a boat launch on Lake Erie.

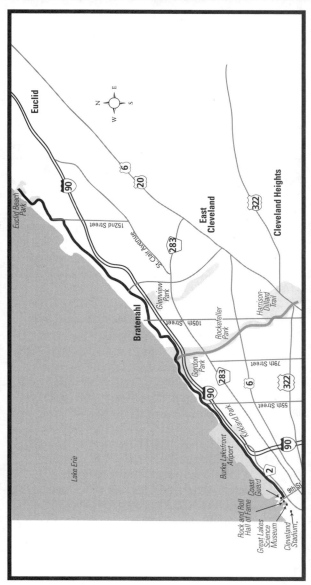

Contact and Tourist Information:

Brooke Fischbach
Cleveland Lakefronts State Park
8701 Lakeshore Blvd., NE
Cleveland, OH 44108-1069
216-881-8141
cleveland.parks@mail.osp.ee.net

Cleveland Metroparks

Cuyahoga

State of Project: Open
End Points: 15 Metroparks
Reservations
Length: 81 miles
Surface: Asphalt

Cleveland Metroparks comprise a system of reservations linked together to form a green loop often called the "Emerald Necklace." There are more than 20,000 acres of land in 15 reservations, connecting parkways and the Cleveland Metroparks Zoo, including more than 80 miles of paved all-purpose trails.

An all-purpose trail begins in the Rocky River Reservation at Detroit Road and travels through the entire reservation. From there, it links to the Mill Stream Run Reservation. The trail travels a continuous 22 miles. There is an offshoot to the Big Creek Reservation from Valley Parkway near Pearl Road. The trail in Big Creek Reservation continues 7.5 miles to Brookpark Road.

At the end of Mill Stream Run Reservation, the trail continues 2.9 miles into the Brecksville Reservation. It is possible to follow Valley Parkway to Route 21 to link up with the trail again for four more miles to Riverview Road and linking with the Ohio & Erie Canalway Towpath Trail (page 70). North of Rockside Road, the Canalway continues from the Cuyahoga Valley National Park north 7.5 miles through the Ohio & Erie Canal Reservation to Old Harvard Road.

Parking and trail access are available in any of the reservation parks.

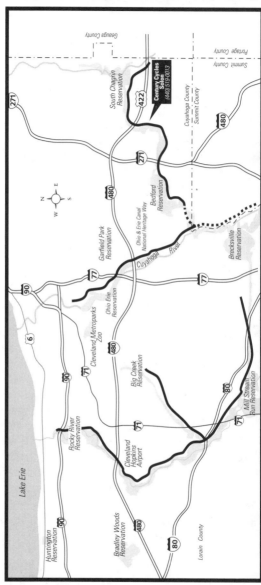

Contact and Tourist Information:

Cleveland Metroparks
Visitor Services
4101 Fulton Parkway
Cleveland, OH 44144-1923
216-635-3238
www.clemetparks.com

Harrison Dillard Bikeway

Cuyahoga

State of Project: Open
End Points: Lake Erie (N) and Case Western Reserve University (S)
Length: 3.6 miles
Surface: Asphalt

The Harrison Dillard Bikeway is a north-south urban path that not only connects the Lake Erie shoreline with the University Circle district, but connects the trail user with Cleveland's cultural past. Beginning at Gordon Park, where the trail links with the Cleveland Lakefront Bikeway (page 64), it follows Martin Luther King Jr. Boulevard south through historic Rockefeller Park and its many cultural gardens. The path is on both sides of the road, offering the user many sights of fascinating historic gardens, elegant arched bridges, and Victorian houses.

At east 105th Street, the bikeway becomes an asphalt path through the University Circle area until it reaches Case Western Reserve University and the Red Line Rapid Transit Station. At Euclid Avenue, the trail user may go a short distance to the east to the Cleveland Museum of Art, the Cleveland Botanical Gardens, and many other cultural attractions in the immediate area.

Plans are for the trail to extend to the eastern suburbs of Shaker Heights and Beachwood.

Visitors can find parking at the Cleveland Lakefront State Park, approximately two-tenths of a mile from the north terminus of the trail. Follow the signs from the parking area to the trailhead. At the south terminus of the trail parking can be found just north of the Martin Luther King Jr. Boulevard and East 105th Street intersection at the Rockefeller Park Lagoon.

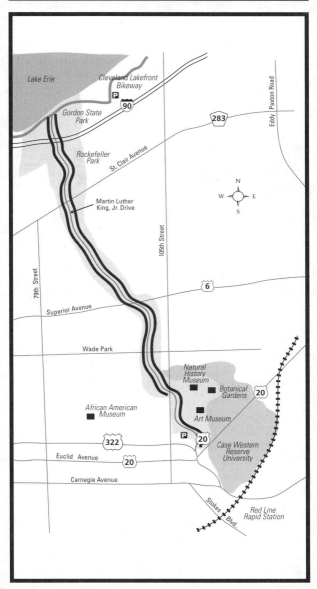

Contact and Tourist Information:

City of Cleveland
Department of Parks
and Recreation
500 Lakeside Avenue
Cleveland, OH 44114
216-664-2484

Ohio & Erie Canalway Towpath Trail

Cuyahoga, Summit, Stark, Tuscarawas

State of Project: Partially open
End Points: Harvard Road (N)
and Route 212 (S)
Length: 101 miles
Surface: Mixed

This trail follows the historic route of the Ohio and Erie Canal through the Ohio & Erie National Heritage Canalway. The canal was built between 1825 and 1832 to provide a transportation route from Cleveland, to Portsmouth. Today the Ohio & Erie Canalway Towpath Trail offers runners, hikers, cyclists, and others a place of peace and tranquility. Canal locks can still be seen along the trail, and interpretive signs explain the canal's features and significance.

A segment of the cross-state Ohio to Erie Trail (page 34), the trail takes users into the Cleveland area through Stark, Summit, and Tuscarawas Counties. Meadows, forests, beaver ponds, and wetlands are visible along the trail, which also offers picnic areas, restrooms, and access points to the Cuyahoga Valley Scenic Railroad. The Cuyahoga Valley National Park logs approximately two million visits a year to the accessible portion of the trail.

Currently, 71 of the proposed 101 miles are open for use. Construction is ongoing. Visitors may stop at visitor centers within the Ohio & Erie Canal National Heritage Canalway or contact the Cuyahoga Valley National Park for more information.

Parking may be found all along the trail, but visitors to the area may wish to park and access the trail in the Cuyahoga Valley National Park in Cuyahoga County, along State Route 8 south of Interstate 480.

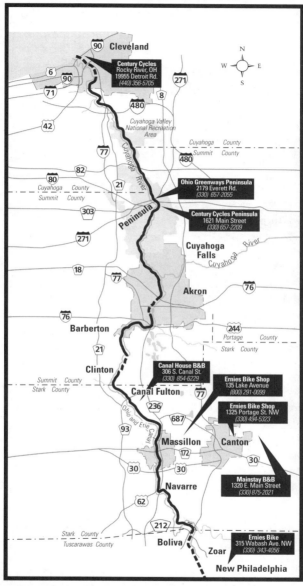

Contact and Tourist Information:

Cuyahoga Valley
National Park
216-524-1497
www.nps.gov/cuva

Cleveland Metroparks
216-351-6300
www.clemetparks.com

Metro Parks, Serving
Summit County
330-867-5511
www.summitmetroparks.org

Stark County Park District
330-477-3552
www.starkparks.com

Tuscarawas County
Ohio & Erie Canalway
Coalition
330-434-5657
www.ohioeriecanal.org

Ohio to Erie Trail Delaware County

Delaware

State of Project: Partially open
End Points: Delaware Knox Co. line (E) and Maxtown Road (SW)
Length: 13.5 miles
Surface: Asphalt

This segment of the Ohio to Erie Trail follows the former 3C rail line, the historic connection between Cincinnati and Cleveland through Columbus. This trail will be a part of the northern, or "Heart of Ohio," route of the Ohio to Erie Trail (page 34).

Beginning near the Delaware and Franklin County line at the northern edge of the Westerville Bikeway (page 88), this trail continues north through the township of Genoa and the Villages of Galena and Sunbury as it continues on to the Delaware and Knox County line, linking with the Heart of Ohio Trail (page 122).

Parking facilities are available for the current trail segment in Genoa Township at the intersection of Big Walnut Road and State Route 3 at McNamara Park.

Photo: A. Holmes

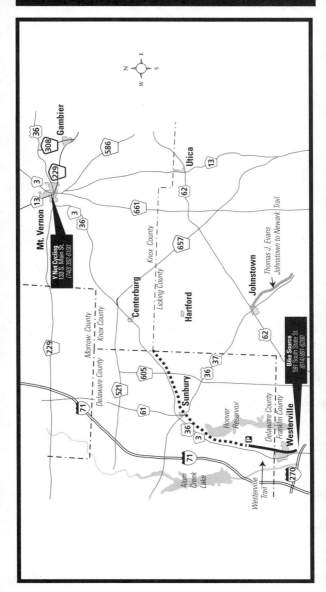

Contact and Tourist Information:

Mike O'Neil, President
Delaware County
Friends of the Trail
P. O. Box 2302
Westerville, OH 43082
moneill@cscc.edu

Mary Kerr, Vice President
Delaware County
Friends of the Trail
mkerr@otterbein.edu

Delaware

State of Project: Planned
End Points: Winter and Lake Streets (E) and Boulder and Houk Roads (W)
Length: 4 miles
Surface: Asphalt

The City of Delaware Recreation Department's planned trail will be constructed along the former CSX rail line that once connected Delaware to Marysville. The four-mile trail system will take the user across the Olentangy River and US Route 23, over the same 500-foot steel train bridge that once carried locomotives and boxcars. Adjacent to the campus of Ohio Wesleyan University, the trail provides a route through the historic downtown district and links with two elementary schools and other destination points around town.

Ohio Wesleyan University students have joined in a cooperative effort with city officials to plan and build this trail. Such cooperation creates not only a wonderful trail for local citizens and visitors to enjoy the beauty of the city, but also educates future planners and engineers about the value of preserving the right-of-way of former rail lines and the creation of freely accessible, multi-use transportation corridors.

Plans call for the construction of the first 1.5 miles of trail in 2005. The entire trail will be available for use in 2007. Parking facilities are available at Winter Street, Liberty Street, and Houk Road Park.

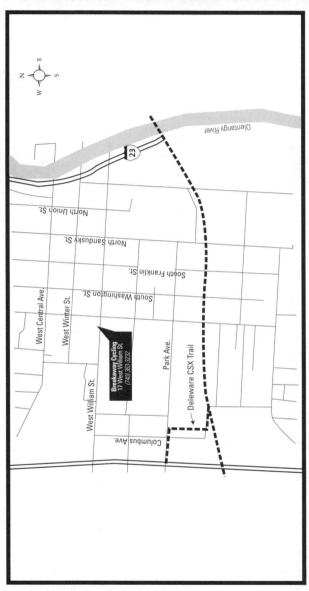

Contact and Tourist Information:

Randy L. Smith
Director,
City of Delaware Department of Recreation Services
1 South Sandusky Street
Delaware, OH 43015
rsmith@delawareohio.net
www.delawareohio.net

Erie

State of Project: Partially open
End Points: DuPont Marsh and
Mason Road (N) and Main Street (S)
Length: 12.8 miles
Surface: Gravel

The Huron River Greenway offers the user primarily natural, undeveloped scenic beauty. Much of the area is zoned as a flood plain, so development potential is limited. The greenway has many interesting historic sites, including the Thomas Edison Museum in Milan. There are bridges and an observation shelter for bird watching over an extensive wetland area.

The Milan Canal route was a vital transportation route for many years. Native Americans, trappers, traders, missionaries, and ocean-bound ships all came along the bustling Milan Canal. Eventually the canal gave way to the rail lines following the old canal and providing Ohioans a connection to the Great Lakes.

Currently, the trail is not continuous. Signs are provided to guide users around the unavailable segment. Future plans call for developing the trail south, eventually linking into the city of Norwalk.

Visitors will find parking at the DuPont Marsh State Nature Preserve parking lot, along River Road off of State Route 2, as well as in the north and south side parking lots on Mason Road. Visitors may use State Route 13 to Mason Road to reach parking along the north side of the trail, or River Road to Mason Road to find the south side parking.

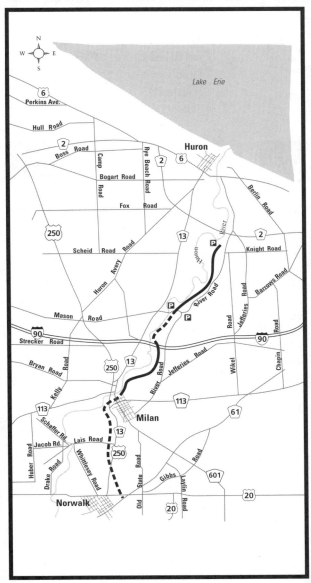

Contact and Tourist Information:

Erie MetroParks
3910 Perkins Avenue
Huron, OH 44839
419-625-7783
discoverit@eriemetroparks.org

Steven Myers
Huron River Greenway Coalition
4614 Barrington Club Drive
Columbus, OH 43220
614-457-7341
hrgc@compuserve.com

Fairfield

State of Project: Partially open
End Points: Lanreco Park (E) and
Ohio University Lancaster (W)
Length: 79.4 miles
Surface: Asphalt and gravel

Currently this county network of trails offers trail users 3.3 miles of the planned 79.4 miles. This trail will eventually be an extensive system that will connect parks, schools, and communities. When complete, this trail network will provide an east-west corridor through growing Fairfield County.

From the Historical Society Museum in Bremen, the trail utilizes former rail corridor, taking users south of downtown Lancaster Heritage District under US Route 33. Continuing west, the trail passes Cenci Lake Park and Talmadge Elementary School, coming within blocks of Martens Park and then on to the Olivedale Senior Citizens Center. A short connector trail exists from Cenci Lake Park to Olivedale.

Continuing westbound and exiting Lancaster, the trail will pass Shallenberger State Nature Preserve where one may view Blackhand sandstone knobs, wildflowers, and old-growth hardwoods. On to historic Amanda, after passing Amanda-Clear Creek School, the trail will cross Clear Creek and continue on to Stoutsville.

Parking and trail access for the currently available trail segment may be found at Ohio University – Lancaster. Visitors may take US Route 33 to State Route 37 north. Continue to the Lancaster campus of Ohio University; the trail is available along the east side of campus.

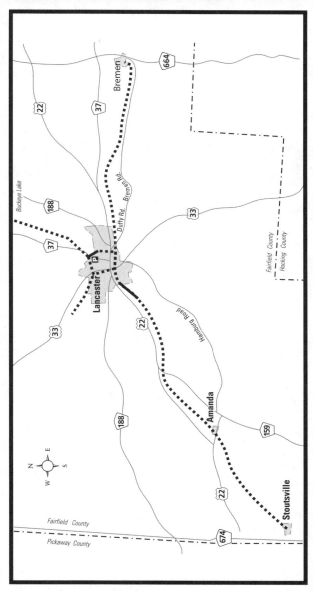

Contact and Tourist Information:

Dr. Jim Barrett, President
Fairfiled Heritage
Trail Association
P. O. Box 765
Lancaster, OH 43130
740-687-1623
barrettj29@hotmail.com

Jeff Vandervoort, V.P.
Fairfield Heritage
Trail Association
P. O. Box 765
Lancaster, OH 43130
740-653-0461
jkv@sitvanlaw.com

Ira Weiss, Secretary
Fairfield Heritage
Trail Association
P. O. Box 765
Lancaster, OH 43130
614-864-0808
iweiss@insight.rr.com

www.lancaster-oh.com/Heritage

Tri-County Triangle Trail

Fayette, Highland, Ross

State of Project: Partially open
End Points: Washington Court House (NW), Austin (S), Chillicothe (SE), and Greenfield (SW)
Length: 52 miles
Surface: Asphalt

The Tri-County Triangle Trail will connect Chillicothe, Frankfort, Washington Court House, and Greenfield with a 52-mile converted rail-trail through three counties primarily along the former CSX/B&O Railroad corridor. Currently, approximately 14 miles of trail, in four segments, is open for use. In addition, nearly 6.5 miles of trail from Washington Court House southeast toward Austin are open. Hikers, walkers, and some bicycles are able to utilize this segment at this time. The asphalt surface is expected to be completed by 2006. The remainder of the trail will be completed

as funds are available.

Parking for the longest, currently open trail segment may be found outside of Chillicothe at Sulpher Lick Road. Visitors may take US Route 50 to Veterans Parkway, turn left onto Anderson Station Road, proceed to Maple Grove Road, turn right and then immediately left onto Sulpher Lick Road and into the parking area. There is additional parking at the Brad Lightle Park in Frankfort.

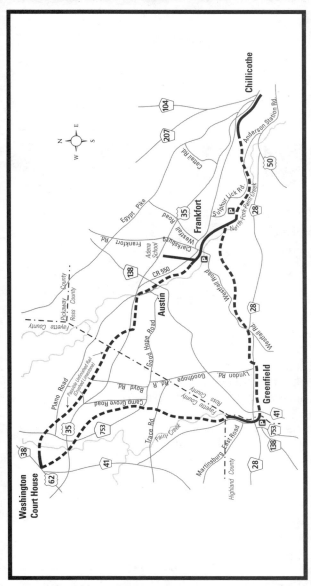

Contact and Tourist Information:

Gary Merkamp, Director
Ross County Park District
15 North Paint Street
Chillicothe, OH 45601
740-773-8794
littpark@bright.net
www.rosscountyparkdistrict.com

Tri-County Triangle Trail, Inc.
P. O. Box 887
Chillicothe, OH 45601
740-774-3008

Alum Creek Multi-Use Trail

Franklin

State of Project: Partially open
End Points: Westerville (N) and
Three Creeks Park (S)
Length: 22 miles
Surface: Asphalt

This urban multi-use trail follows a north-south route along Alum Creek, through neighborhoods and commercial areas as well as parks. It links with the Westerville Bikeway (page 88) at the north terminus and Three Creeks Park at the south terminus. In addition, future plans are to link with the I-670 Trail (page 84), Big Walnut, and Blacklick Creek Trails.

The Alum Creek Multi-Use Trail is a segment along the cross-state Ohio to Erie Trail (page 34) that will connect Cincinnati with Cleveland through Columbus.

Parking and access to the open segments of the trail are available at the Westerville Recreation Center, Cooper Park, and Gasto Park along the six-mile northern section. Wolf Park on Main Street in Bexley offers parking for users of the mid-section of the trail. In 2005, trail users will be able to park at the Three Creeks Park and access the trail directly.

Photo: A. Holmes

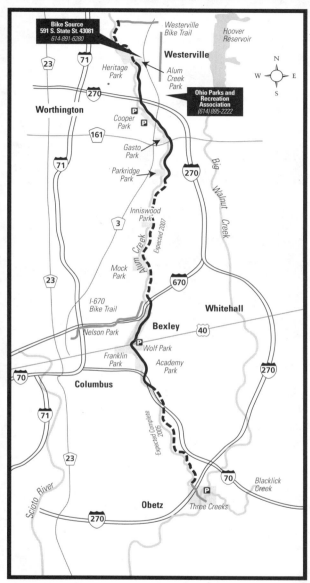

Contact and Tourist Information:

Brad Westall
Columbus Recreation
and Parks Deparment
200 West Greenlawn
Columbus, OH 43223
614-645-3300
www.columbusrecparks.com

Franklin

State of Project: Open
End Points: Airport Drive (E) and Cleveland Avenue (W)
Parking: Fort Hayes Park
Length: 3 miles
Surface: Asphalt

Trail users may currently use the I-670 Bikeway to travel from Ohio Dominican College at Airport Drive to the Fort Hayes Park on Cleveland Avenue.

The I-670 Bikeway is an urban connector trail that will eventually link with the Alum Creek Multi-Use Trail (page 82) to the east and the Olentangy/Lower Scioto Multi-Use Trail (page 86) under the Nationwide Arena to the west. Trail access and parking are available at Fort Hayes Park along State Route 3.

Photo: A. Holmes

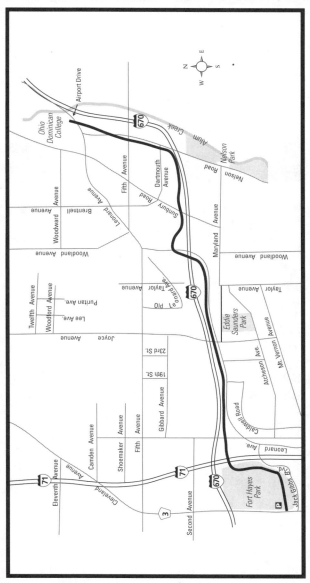

Contact and Tourist Information:

Brad Westall
Columbus Recreation and Parks Deparment
200 West Greenlawn
Columbus, OH 43223
614-645-3300
www.columbusrecparks.com

Olentangy/Lower Scioto Multi-Use Trail

Franklin

State of Project: Open
End Points: Worthington Hills Park (N) and SR 104 (S)
Length: 18 miles
Surface: Asphalt

This is an urban/suburban trail through residential, commercial, and parkland areas. It provides a scenic route along the Olentangy and Lower Scioto Rivers through Columbus. This popular trail provides access to numerous parks that have additional trails within them, as well as many other recreational opportunities. The Olentangy/Lower Scioto Multi-Use Trail serves as both a recreation and a transportation system, providing north-south access through the city west of State Route 23. Residents use the trail as a commuter path for work and leisure.

The final construction of the trail will be a link with the I-670 Bikeway (page 84) that will provide a connection to the Alum Creek Multi-Use Trail (page 82).

Parking is available north of Interstate 270 at Worthington Hills Park and on the south side of Interstate 270 at Wilson-Bridge Road in Worthington. Trail users may also find parking and access to the corridor at Olentangy Nature Park, Anheuser Busch Sports Park, and Northmoor Park along Olentangy River Road. Tuttle Park, north of Lane Avenue and west of US Route 23, also has parking. Berliner Park, along the west banks of the Lower Scioto River, north of State Route104, and at State Route104 along the east bank of the river, provides parking for the south terminus of the trail.

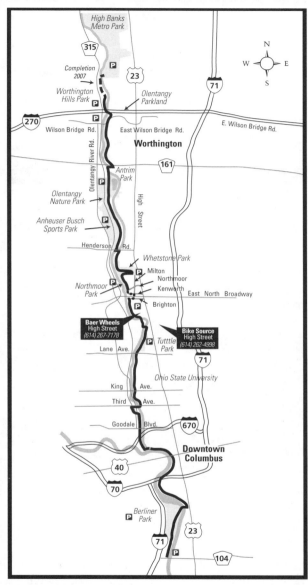

Contact and Tourist Information:

Brad Westall
Columbus Recreation and Parks Deparment
200 West Greenlawn
Columbus, OH 43223
614-645-3300
www.columbusrecparks.com

Westerville Bikeway

Franklin

State of Project: Open
End Points: Maxtown Road (N)
and Schrock Road (S)
Length: 2.7 miles
Surface: Asphalt

The Westerville Bikeway is a 2.7-mile trail that utilizes former Conrail Railroad corridor between Schrock Road and Maxtown Road and is a segment of the Ohio to Erie Trail (page 34).

The first section of the trail from Maxtown Road to Old County Line Road was completed in 1998. In 1999, the trail was extended south to State Street.

Current plans are for the trail to cross Maxtown Road in 2005, head north and link with the Ohio to Erie Trail Delaware County (page 72) in Genoa Township. In 2006, Westerville Bikeway will link to the south with the Schrock Road bike lane, a designated on-road route, which connects trail users with the Alum Creek Multi-Use Trail (page 82).

Parking and trail access are available at Hoff Woods Park located at 556 McCorkle Boulevard and at the Recreation Program Center at 64 East Walnut Street.

Photo: A. Holmes

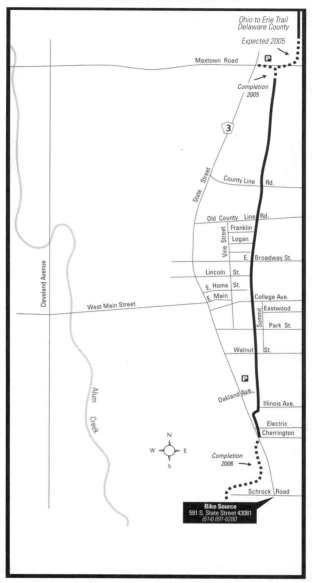

Contact and Tourist Information:

Michael Hooper
Westerville Parks and Recreation
350 N. Cleveland Avenue
Westerville, OH 43082
614-901-6500
mhooper@ci.westerville.oh.us
www.westerville.org

Franklin, Madison

State of Project: Open
End Points: Cemetery Pike Road (NW) and Downtown Hilliard (SE)
Length: 8 miles
Surface: Blacktop

The Heritage Rail Trail provides the community with an eight-mile safe transportation route from historic downtown Hilliard to Cemetery Pike, approximately 1.5 miles out from Plain City. A part of the Ohio to Erie Trail (page 34), the Heritage Rail Trail is a beautiful corridor for year-round recreation. Picnic facilities, playgrounds, and restrooms are available at the Homestead Park along the trail.

The Columbus Metro Parks' administered staging area at Hayden Run Road offers a large parking area, horse corral, and wetlands area. The trail is open for horseback riding from Hayden Run Road to Cemetery Pike. The Hayden Run trailhead is on Hayden Run Road west of Cosgray Road at approximately mid-trail from downtown Hilliard. From Interstate 270 exit onto Tuttle Road, continue toward Wilcox Road and turn left. Follow Wilcox Road to Hayden Run Road and turn right. Proceed approximately 2.75 miles. The trailhead is on the right.

To reach the trailhead in downtown Hilliard, exit Interstate 270 at Cemetery Road to Hilliard. Go west on Cemetery Road to Main Street. Turn right at Main Street and continue north to Center Street. Turn left at Center Street into the trailhead parking lot. Currently, there are no parking facilities at the northwest end of the trail at Cemetery Pike.

Future plans are to extend the trail south to Leap Road and link with the city of Columbus trail system. To the north, the possibility of extending the trail into Plain City is being considered.

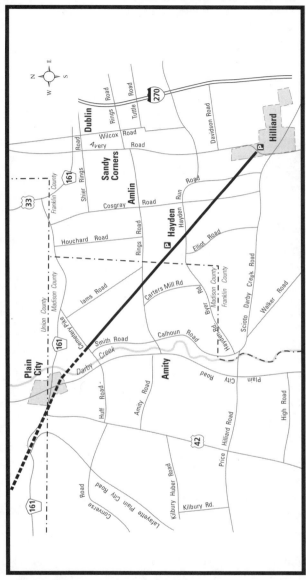

Contact and Tourist Information:

Leonard Fisher, President
Heritage Rail-Trail Coalition
2020 Parklawn Drive
Hilliard, OH 43026
Homestead Park 614-876-9554
information@heritagerailtrail.org
www.heritagerailtrail.org

Janell Thomas, Director
Washington Township Parks
4675 Cosgray Road
Hilliard, OH 43026
614-876-9554
thomasj@washingtontownship.oh.us

Wabash Cannonball Trail

Fulton, Henry, Lucas, Williams

State of Project: Partially open
End Points: Maumee (E), Montpelier (W) and Liberty Center (S)
Length: 64 miles
Surface: Asphalt and ballast

The Wabash Cannonball Trail is a linear park on two former railroad corridors: one east to west from Maumee to near Montpelier, and one southwest from Maumee to Liberty Center. In 2005, the trail segment from west of Wauseon to West Unity will be completed when the last culverts are installed, adding an additional 15 miles to the two miles of available trail. From the break in the trail east of Wauseon, it is possible to ride on road to where the trail picks up again at State Route 109, about a mile south of Delta. With a total of 16 bridges, this trail is a scenic beauty.

The trail surface in Lucas County is asphalt; in Fulton, Williams and Henry Counties the surface is cinder ballast. Bicycles may travel upon cinder ballast. For additional information, please contact the trail organization.

Visitors to the trail may find parking and trail access at Monclova Community Center, located at Monclova Road and Lose Road off of US Route 24. Parking is also available in the Village of Whitehouse, Oak Opening Metropark, and at the trailhead south of Delta on State Route 109.

Photo: Gene Markley

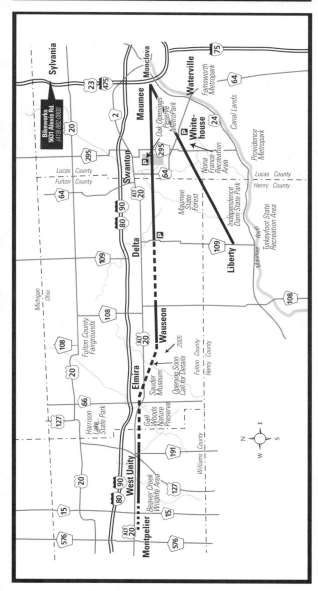

Contact and Tourist Information:

Northwestern
Ohio Rails-to-Trails Association, Inc.
P. O. Box 234
Delta, OH 43515
1-800-951-4788 or 419-822-4788
www.wabashcannonballtrail.org

Gallia

State of Project: Partially open
End Points: Minerton (N) and
Kanauga (S)
Length: 25 miles
Surface: Smooth, crushed gravel

The Gallia County Bikeway begins in the heart of Gallipolis, connecting parks, schools, a nursing home facility, hospital, golf course, and commercial and residential areas. Winding north from downtown, the trail offers a scenic route through hilly terrain, while the grade remains quite flat.

This former CSX railroad right-of-way includes historic points of interest such as the Bidwell Depot Site, a stop on the Underground Railroad, a marker commemorating the Stone Water Towers, and the historic depot in Gallipolis.

Currently, two sections of the trail are available for use. One begins in Gallipolis and is 2.5 miles and the other is 4.5 miles beginning in Kerr.

Future plans for trail facilities include refurbishing the historic depot in Gallipolis.

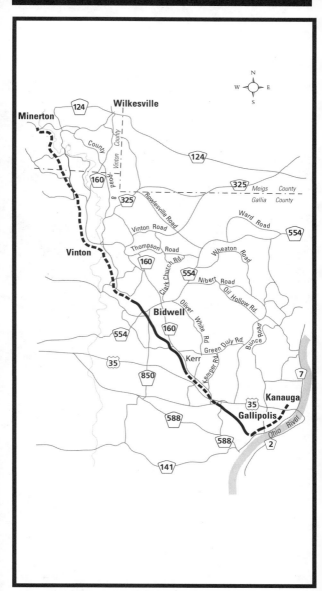

Contact and Tourist Information:

Amy Bowman-Moore
O.O. McIntyre Park District
18 Locust Street, Room 1262
Gallipolis, OH 45631-1262
740-446-4612 x 254
amymoore@gallianet.net

Geauga

State of Project: Partially open
End Points: Geauga and
Lake County line (N) and
Headwaters Park (S)
Length: 20.2 miles
Surface: Asphalt

The Maple Highlands Trail consists of three separate sections. The 4.2-mile north section was opened in 2003. The construction of the central section, which runs from the City of Chardon to Headwaters Park, is expected to take place in 2005. These two federally funded phases will stretch a distance of 12.5 miles. A third southern-most section, running 7.7 miles from Headwaters Park to the Geauga and Trumbull County line, is planned for the future.

The path will treat trail users to scenic views of forests, wetlands, natural meadows and farmlands of Geauga County as it crosses the headwater streams of the Cuyahoga River.

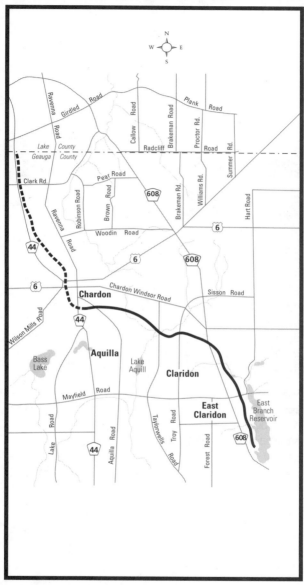

Contact and Tourist Information:

Paige Hosier
Geauga Park District
9160 Robinson Road
Chardon, OH 44024
440-286-9516
800-536-4006
info@geaugaparkdistrict.org
www.geaugaparkdistrict.org

Creekside Trail

Greene, Montgomery

State of Project: Open
End Points: Xenia Station (E) and Eastwood MetroPark (W)
Length: 15.1 miles
Surface: Asphalt

The Creekside Trail follows the Shawnee Creek from the Xenia area and continues to Beavercreek following the Little and Big Beaver Creeks. Meandering along the peaceful creeks under the shade of trees, it is bordered by two wetland areas that provide views of rare plants and animals. Utilizing the 140-foot bridge over Shawnee Creek at James Ranch, trail enthusiasts are able to commute to the Fairgrounds Recreation Center Park, Mullins Pool, the Greene County Fairgrounds, and the Little Miami Scenic Trail (page 54).

The trail continues from the Greene/Montgomery County line and connects with the Five Rivers MetroParks trail system. This provides connections with the RT8/Mad River Recreation Trail (page 158), and the RT7/Stillwater River Recreation Trail (page 160). In Montgomery County, the Creekside Trail is also known as RT 2/Creekside Recreational Trail.

Parking and trail access may be found at the trail's east terminus at Xenia Station (page 106), off of US Route 68, as well as along the trail at Alpha, Nutter Park, Grange Hall Road, Fifth/Third Gateway Park off of US Route 35, and the west terminus at Eastwood MetroPark.

Photo: www.miamivalleytrails.org

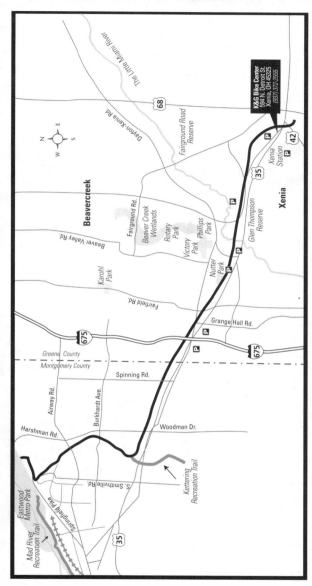

Contact and Tourist Information:

Jim Schneider, Trail Manager
Greene County Parks and Recreation
651 Dayton - Xenia Road
Xenia, OH 45385
937-562-7440
jschneider@co.greene.oh.us

Craig Wenner, Operations Manager
Five Rivers MetroParks
1375 East Siebenthaler Avenue
Dayton, OH 45414
937-278-8231
cwenner@metroparks.org
www.metroparks.org

Greene

State of Project: Open
End Points: Central Avenue (N) and Skyline Drive (S)
Length: 4.3 miles
Surface: Asphalt and concrete

This bikeway provides a connection from Fairborn to Wright State University and is a part of the statewide Buckeye Trail. Future plans include extending the trail across State Route 444 to Huffman Prairie Flying Field Hanger and Wright Patterson Air Force Base. This link will connect the Dayton trail system and the Greene County trail system through the RT8/Mad River Recreation Trail (page 158).

Fairborn's Wright Brothers Huffman Prairie Bikeway

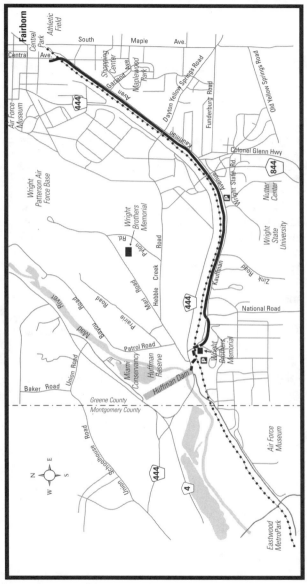

Contact and Tourist Information:

Jim Schneider, Trail Manager
Greene County Parks and Recreation
651 Dayton - Xenia Road
Xenia, OH 45385
937-562-7440
jschneider@co.greene.oh.us

Greene

State of Project: Partially open
End Points: Jamestown
Length: 11 miles
Surface: Asphalt

The Jamestown Connector currently offers trail users 7.5 miles of trail from Jamestown toward Xenia. The project is being built in phases from Jamestown to Xenia and will eventually link with the Xenia Station (page 106). In the other direction, plans are for additional trail to connect with Washington Court House and the Tri-County Triangle Trail (page 80). Once both trails are complete, trail users will be able to travel from Xenia Station to Washington Court House, Circleville, Lancaster, and Bremen.

Trail visitors to the current trail may find parking at the Frank Seaman Park in Jamestown.

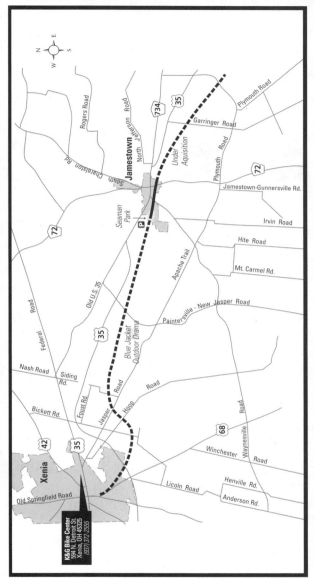

Contact and Tourist Information:

Jim Schneider, Trail Manager
Greene County Parks and Recreation
651 Dayton - Xenia Road
Xenia, OH 45385
937-562-7440
jschneider@co.greene.oh.us

Greene

State of Project: Partially open
End Points: Cedarville (E) and
Xenia Station (W)
Length: 7.8 miles
Surface: Asphalt

This segment of the Ohio to Erie Trail (page 34), that will connect Cincinnati and Cleveland through Columbus, passes quickly from the urban setting of Xenia into the beautiful rural setting of Greene County. Along the way there is a nine-tenths of a mile link to Central State University, Wilberforce University, and the National Afro-American Museum. The trail traverses fertile farmlands, continues over a magnificent wooded gorge with limestone cliffs, and passes through a mature hardwood forest, linking the Bob Evans Park and Lexington Park in Xenia and the Cedarville Community Park in Cedarville.

The trail links with the Prairie Grass Trail (page 56), another section of the Ohio to Erie Trail, in Cedarville.

Parking and Trail access are available at Xenia Station and Cedarville.

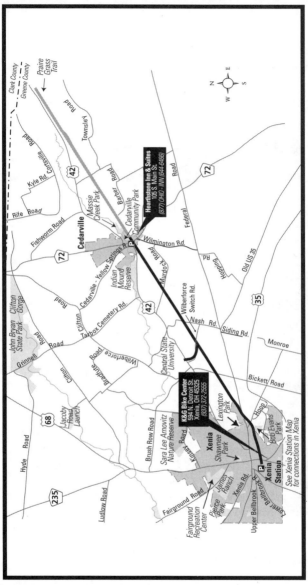

Contact and Tourist Information:

Jim Schneider, Trail Manager
Greene County Parks and Recreation
651 Dayton - Xenia Road
Xenia, OH 45385
937-562-7440
jschneider@co.greene.oh.us
www.co.greene.oh.us

Xenia Station

Greene

State of Project: Open
End Points: Xenia
Surface: Asphalt

Xenia Station, once a railroad hub, is now a trail hub. Located on the site of an old depot that includes a replica of a nineteenth-century railroad building, it houses restrooms, concessions, displays, bike patrol headquarters, an effective cycling training classroom, and a visitor information center. In the future, trail managers plan to include equipment rental facilities.

The trails that meet in Xenia are all marked by signs. Trail #1 is marked with both Springfield and Spring Valley. The Springfield direction is the north section of the Little Miami Scenic Trail (page 54), and the Spring Valley direction is the south section of the Little Miami Scenic Trail (page 54). Trail #2 is the Creekside Trail (page 98), which takes trail users toward Dayton and links with the Eastwood MetroPark. Trail #3 is the Jamestown Connector (page 102). Not currently built, the trail will offer users a link with Jamestown, 11 miles away, and then connect with Washington Court House. Trail #4 is the Ohio to Erie Trail Greene County segment (page 104). This segment of the cross-state trail from Cincinnati to Cleveland through Columbus connects with the Prairie Grass Trail (page 56) in Cedarville, continuing on to London in Madison County.

Xenia Station is accessible in Xenia along US Route 68. Xenia Station serves as a parking hub for the many trails that link within its confines.

Contact and Tourist Information:

Jim Schneider, Trail Manager
Greene County Parks and Recreation
651 Dayton - Xenia Road
Xenia, OH 45385
937-562-7440
jschneider@co.greene.oh.us
www.co.greene.oh.us

California Junction Trail

Hamilton

State of Project: Open
End Points: Loop Trail
Length: 1 mile
Surface: Dirt

The California Junction Trail is one of two National Recreation Trails located in the 115-acre California Woods Nature Preserve. Located near the mouth of the Little Miami and Ohio Rivers, the former rail line was operated by the Cincinnati, Georgetown & Portsmouth Railroad. California Junction served as a switch station, a compulsory stop for all crews to receive instructions. The line served the areas between Georgetown, Batavia, and Columbia. Train service ended in 1939.

This trail is a one-mile circuit-loop on the highest point of elevation in the preserve. Since the last train ran, the woodlands have become a mature hardwood forest with a variety of oak, hickory, maple, and beech. Wildlife abounds and a variety of wildflowers blanket the hidden remains of concrete trestle pillars and rail bed fragments which link the trail to the past.

Parking is available at the California Woods Nature Preserve parking, accessible from US Route 52 to Park Road.

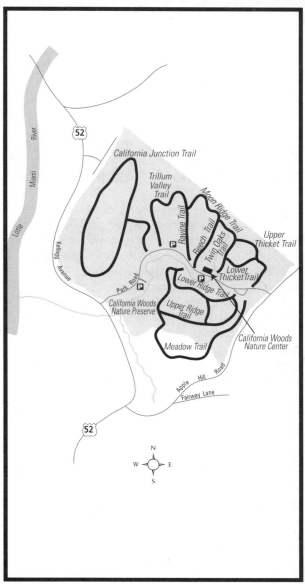

Contact and Tourist Information:

Jim Farfsing
Director of Education
Cincinnati Parks
4 Beech Lane
Cincinnati, OH 45208
513-321-6070
jim.farfsing@cincinnati-oh.gov

Mill Creek Greenway

Hamilton

State of Project: Planned
End Points: Hamilton (N) and
the Ohio River (S)
Length: 28 miles
Surface: Undecided

The Mill Creek Greenway System promotes the restoration, preservation and enhancement of Mill Creek and its tributaries, a degraded urban stream that runs through the geographic heart of Cincinnati in southwest Ohio. The entire Mill Creek Greenway Trail will be approximately 28 miles and has the potential to expand throughout the 166-square-miles of the watershed area. The greenway system is comprised of primary and secondary stream corridors supplemented by parks, utility corridors, and open spaces to form an interconnected system of "multi-objective corridors" throughout the watershed. Work has already begun on a number of pilot projects representing nearly ten miles of proposed multi-use trails.

The Mill Creek Watershed Greenway System will provide recreational opportunities and transportation alternatives for citizens. It will also improve floodplain management and water quality within the primary and tributary channels of Mill Creek, and contribute to the economic well-being of the Greater Cincinnati metropolitan region.

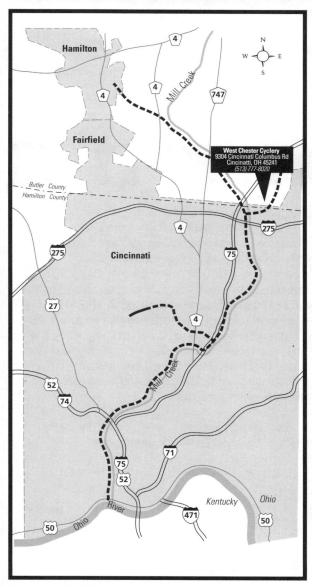

Contact and Tourist Information:

Mill Creek Restoration Project
1617 Elmore Court
Cincinnati, OH 45223
513-731-8400
info@millcreekrestoration.org
www.millcreekrestoration.org

Hancock

State of Project: Open
End Points: Bright Road and County Road 95 (E), and I-75 bridge (W)
Length: 7.73 miles
Surface: Asphalt

The Blanchard River Greenway is a segment of the 20-mile Heritage Trail that follows the Blanchard River. A portion of this trail from Howard Street to Main Street lies along the former B&O rail corridor.

The greenway runs through Findlay and is part of the larger Old Mill Stream Parkway (page 114). In Findlay, it is adjacent to parks, a waterfall, Findlay High School, the University of Findlay, and homes and businesses. The trail passes several historic sites, including monuments of the Great Gas Boom at the Karg Well site, Ft. Findlay at Findlay's Main Street Bridge, and Hull's crossing at Riverside during the War of 1812.

Visitors will find parking at the Old Mill Stream Park Visitors Center off East Main Cross Street.

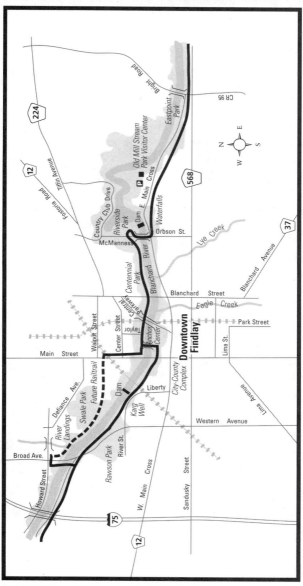

Contact and Tourist Information:

Hancock Park District
1424 East Main Cross Street
Findlay, OH 45840
419-425-7275
www.hancockparks.com

Old Mill Stream Parkway

Hancock

State of Project: Open
End Points: Riverbend (E) and County Road 128 (W)
Length: 18 miles
Surface: Asphalt

The "Old Mill Stream" is the nickname given to the Blanchard River and the many sawmills and grist mills that once lined its banks. The river holds a prominent place in the history of the area and even had a song, "Down by the Old Mill Stream," written about it.

The Old Mill Stream Parkway is a multi-use linear park that runs from Blanchard Landing to Riverbend Recreation area. It follows the Blanchard River, linking several parks, boat access sites, trails, historical areas, and the Blanchard River Greenway (page 112). The Heritage Trail runs through the entire parkway, offering shelters, boat access points, and activity centers.

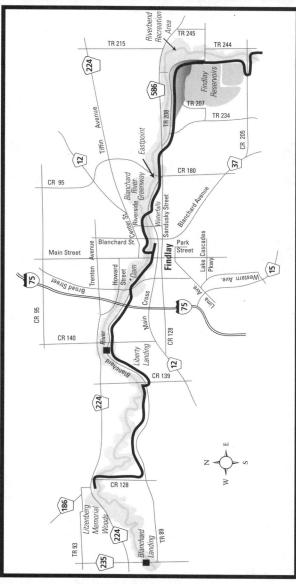

Contact and Tourist Information:

Hancock Park District
1424 East Main Cross Street
Findlay, OH 45840
419-425-7275
www.hancockparks.com

Harrison County Conotton Creek Trail

Harrison

State of Project: Open
End Points: Jewett (E)
and Bowerston (W)
Length: 11.4 miles
Surface: Asphalt

This 11.4-mile multi-use trail in northern Harrison County, and the stream from which its name is derived, meanders through small villages, farmlands, pastures, wetlands, and rolling hills in eastern Ohio. Running parallel to State Route 151, the trail links the villages of Bowerston, Conotton, Scio, and Jewett. Trail users will find parks, local museums, libraries, and access to historic landmarks, including Clark Gable's and General Custer's birthplaces, on or near the trail.

Trail access is available along the trail in each village as well as on County Road 50 between Jewett and Scio off of State Route 151.

Access to the Buckeye Trail (page 24) is also available near Bowerston.

Photo: Chris Copeland

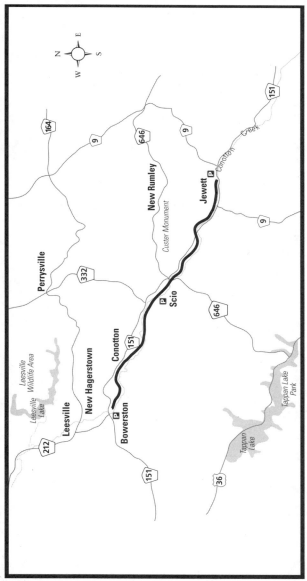

Contact and Tourist Information:

Bob Blanke
P. O. Box 521
Scio, OH 43988
740-945-1761
gilliat1@msn.com
www.harrisoncountyohio.org

Holmes County Trail

Holmes

State of Project: Partially open
End Points: Fredericksburg (N) and Brinkhaven (S)
Length: 29 miles
Surface: Packed crushed limestone

The Holmes County Trail is a 29-mile multi-purpose transportation corridor through southern and western Holmes County that is also a part of the northern leg of the Ohio to Erie Trail (page 34), a cross-state trail connecting Cincinnati with Cleveland through Columbus.

In Brinkhaven, the Holmes County Trail will connect with the Mohican Valley Trail (page 126), continue north through the villages of Glenmont, Killbuck, Millersburg, and Holmesville, and then cross the Wayne County line to the north, ending in Fredericksburg. Along this route, trail users will travel through farmland, woodlands, wetlands, and open fields.

This trail accommodates horse-drawn vehicles that would otherwise have to use dangerous State Route 83, State Route 62 and other township roads to access communities along the trail. It is the first rail-trail in the country open to Amish buggies.

The 3.45 miles of trail from Fredericksburg to Holmesville and 6.67 miles from Holmesville to Millersburg were surfaced with crushed limestone in the summer of 2004. An additional 4.72 miles of rough, primitive earthen trail is available from Millersburg to Killbuck. From Glenmont to Brinkhaven at the Knox County line, rough primitive trail is available for an additional 7.47 miles.

Visitors to the area may find parking in the village of Millersburg.

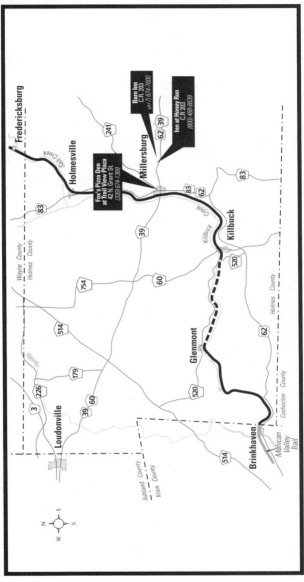

Fredericksburg

Holmesville

Millersburg

Barn Inn
C.R. 203
(617) 674-7600

Inn at Honey Run
C.R. 203
(800) 468-6609

Fox's Pizza Den
at Trail View Plaza
42 N. Grant St.
(330) 674-1369

Killbuck

Glenmont

Brinkhaven

Loudonville

Wayne County
Holmes County

Holmes County
Coshocton County

Ashland County
Knox County

Mohican Valley Trail

Salt Creek

Killbuck Creek

241 83 39 60 754 514 179 226 3 39 60 520 62 520 514 62 83

N
W E
S

Contact and Tourist Information:

Joan Simcack, Director
Holmes County Rails to Trails Coalition
P. O. Box 95
Millersburg, OH 44654
330-279-2643
holmestrail@earthlink.net
www.holmestrail.org

Huron

State of Project: Under construction
End Points: Norwalk (E) and Monroeville (W)
Length: 3.6 miles
Surface: Gravel

Currently, there is a 3.6-mile segment of gravel trail available for use. This trail will open officially in early 2005. There are two particularly beautiful areas where this trail crosses the east and west branches of the Huron River. A part of the greater North Coast Inland Trail (page 30), this trail segment will eventually be joined to the Sandusky (page 176) and Lorain County (page 140) sections. Where possible, the trail utilizes the Toledo, Norwalk, and Cleveland Railroad, established in 1851.

Trail visitors to Huron County will want to exit US Route 20 in Monroeville, turning south to Peru Center Road. Some parking is available in Norwalk at North West Street on the west side of the city.

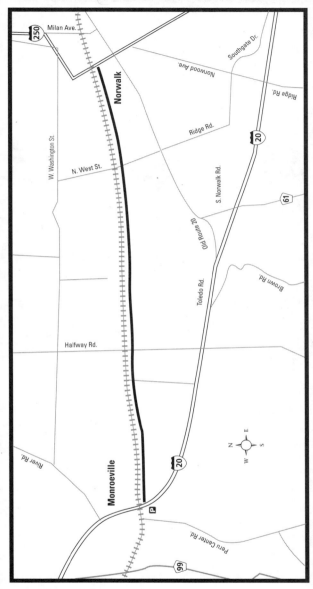

Contact and Tourist Information:

Gordon Oney
Firelands Rails to Trails
P. O. Box 55
North Fairfield, OH 44855
419-744-2458

Heart of Ohio Trail (Ohio to Erie Trail)

Knox County

State of Project: Planned
End Points: Mount Vernon (E) and Delaware Co. line (W)
Length: 16.8 miles
Surface: Asphalt

This segment of the Ohio to Erie Trail follows the former 3C rail line, the historic connection between Cincinnati and Cleveland through Columbus. This trail will be a part of the northern, or "Heart of Ohio" route of the Ohio to Erie Trail (page 34).

Beginning at the Licking County line about three miles southwest of Centerburg, this trail continues north through the Village of Centerburg then on to the City of Mount Vernon, where a future one-mile extension in the village will allow a connection to the Kokosing Gap Trail (page 124).

Parking facilities are available on the street in Centerburg and Mount Vernon.

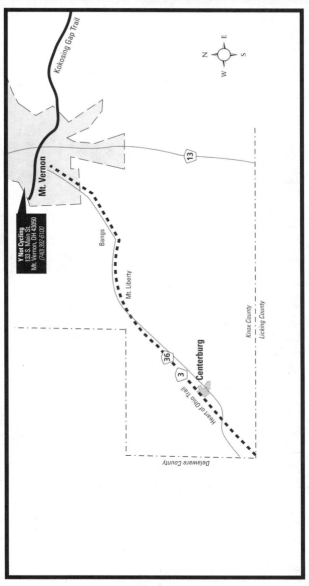

Contact and Tourist Information:

Susan Palmer Cordle, President
Heart of Ohio Trail, Inc.
P. O. Box 16
Centerburg, OH 43011
palmers@kenyon.edu

Knox

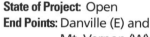

State of Project: Open
End Points: Danville (E) and
Mt. Vernon (W)
Length: 14 miles
Surface: Asphalt

This 14-mile trail utilizes the former Pennsylvania Railroad right-of-way with endpoints in Mount Vernon and Danville. This trail is one of the largest paved rail-trail parks in the United States to be completely donor – and volunteer – maintained.

Along the way from Mount Vernon to Danville, trail users twice cross the Kokosing State Scenic River on railroad bridges more than 250 feet long, and pass through forests, wetlands, farms and villages. In Gambier, visitors will find a restored 1940 ALCO 0-6-0 steam locomotive and a 1924 Chesapeake & Ohio wood caboose on display. Gambier is also home to Kenyon College. It is possible to hike up the hill from the trail to visit the campus. In Howard, children may find enjoyment on a giant playset with a view of a wonderful old stone arch.

The trail is open 24 hours a day, seven days a week, 365 days a year. Water fountains and restrooms are open in Mount Vernon, Gambier, and Howard from mid-April through mid-November. Free electric wheel-chair charging outlets are also available at the picnic shelters in Mount Vernon and Gambier.

The route for the Ohio to Erie Trail (page 34) connects with the Kokosing Gap Trail on the west through Mount Vernon and the Mohican Valley Trail (page 126) on the east.

Parking and trail access are available in Mount Vernon. Take State Route 13 to Mount Vernon Avenue, turn east and continue approximately one mile. Parking will be to the right.

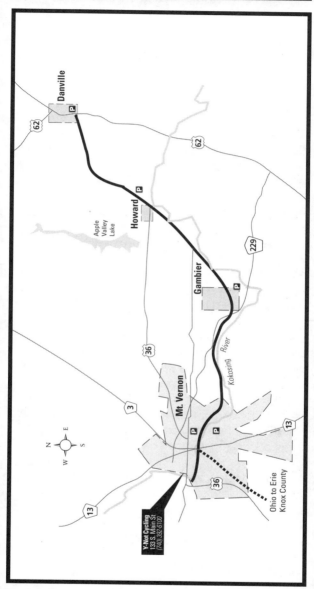

Contact and Tourist Information:

Kokosing Gap Trail
P. O. Box 129
Gambier, OH 43022
740-397-0311 X432
www.kokosinggaptrail.org

Mohican Valley Trail

Knox

State of Project: Open
End Points: Holmes County line (E)
and Danville (W)
Length: 4.8 miles
Surface: Crushed limestone
and dirt

The Mohican Valley Trail follows the old Pennsylvania Railroad corridor beginning in Danville and continues to Brinkhaven at the Holmes County line. It connects to the Mohican River area as well as the Holmes County Trail (page 118) to the east and the Kokosing Gap Trail (page 124) to the west, eventually providing users with about 50 miles of continuous trail.

One of the most striking features of this trail is the "Bridge of Dreams." This beautifully constructed covered bridge stretches 370 feet over the Mohican River. This is the longest covered bridge in Ohio and the second longest in the United States. This trail is an example of how communities work together to provide a multi-use non-motorized trail for cyclists, walkers, horseback riders and Amish buggies.

Parking and trail access for the trail is available at the west terminus of the trail in Danville at East Street, along Buckeye Road about mid-trail, and at Tiger Valley Road off of Mickley Road. Both Buckeye Road and Mickely Road are off of US Route 62. In addition to parking, there is a picnic shelter and water well for humans and horses at the Bridge of Dreams.

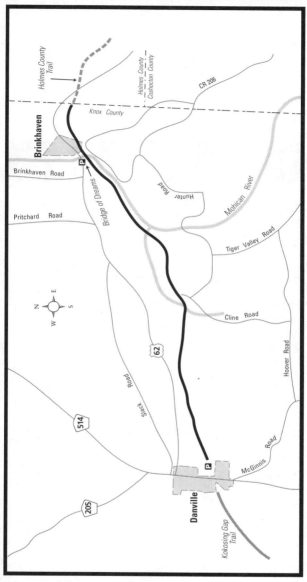

Contact and Tourist Information:

Mohican Valley Trail Board
P. O. Box 261
Howard, OH 43028
740-599-6720

The Owl Creek Trail

Knox

State of Project: Planned
End Points: North of Fredricktown
at SR 95 (N) and Mt. Vernon (S)
Length: 6.37 miles
Surface: Undetermined

The planned 6.37-mile Owl Creek Trail will eventually provide trail users a link from Fredericktown to the Kokosing Gap Trail (page 124) in Mt. Vernon.

Knox County and Fredericktown have held historical significance for many generations. A mound building population once inhabited the area and two mounds are visible from the planned trail along the Kokosing River. Fredericktown is located approximately three miles from the Greenville Treaty Line which opened the Northwest Territory for settlement and expansion westward in 1795. During the 1800s, abolitionist Quakers, active in the Underground Railroad movement, settled in this area of Knox County. More recently, in 1973, Northern Knox County welcomed the establishment of a new Amish community that has grown to more than 160 families. Amish buggies are a common sight along local roadways.

Plans are for parking and trail access to be available at Community Park on the north side of Fredericktown.

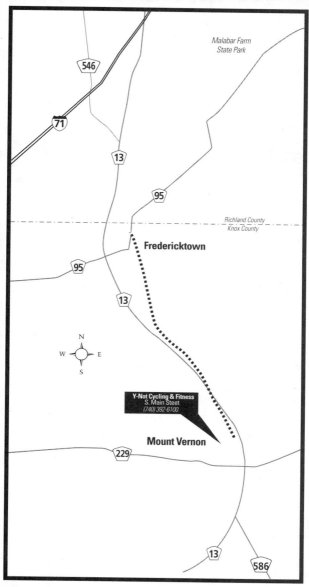

Contact and Tourist Information:

Patricia Stelzer, President
The Owl Creek Trail, Inc.
19 Mohican Drive
Fredericktown, OH 43019
740-694-5280
owlcreektrail@yahoo.com

Lake

State of Project: Partially open
End Points: Jackson Street (N)
and Ravenna Road (S)
Length: 4.5 miles
Surface: Asphalt

Lake Metroparks has converted the railroad right-of-way from the Lake Erie shore to the Geauga County line into a multi-use greenway open to everyone.

This trail connects many parks and schools, providing a scenic and safe route for children and commuters walking, cycling, horseback riding, and cross country skiing.

Parking and trail access at Jackson Street are located approximately one-tenth of a mile north of State Route 20 at George's Dinner Bell, and approximately three-quarters of a mile south of State Route 608 at Ravenna Road.

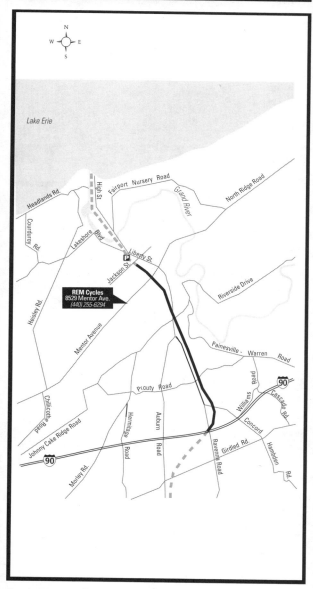

Contact and Tourist Information:

Chuck Kenzig
Lake Metroparks
11211 Spear Road
Concord Township, OH 44077
440-639-7275
ckenzig@lakemetroparks.com
www.lakemetroparks.com

Licking

State of Project: Open
End Points: Toboso (E) and Brushy Fork Road (W)
Length: 4.5 miles
Surface: Asphalt

The Blackhand Gorge is located in the 970-acre Blackhand Gorge State Nature Preserve. The preserve was created in 1975 to ensure that the area's scientific, educational, and aesthetic values will be preserved indefinitely for use by all Ohioans. The prime feature of the preserve is the gorge cut by the Licking River through the Blackhand sandstone formation. The trail follows the river through the gorge and has many quiet side trails to explore.

The name "Blackhand" originated from a large, dark hand-shaped petroglyph that was engraved on the sandstone cliff face. A Native American legend holds that the symbol marked the boundary of a sacred Native American territory where no man was to raise a hand against another. The engraving was destroyed in 1828 during construction of the Ohio to Erie Canal Towpath.

Parking and trail access may be found at the east terminus of the trail at the Main Parking lot off of County Road 273, or the parking lot at the west terminus of the trail along Brushy Fork Road south off of State Route 16.

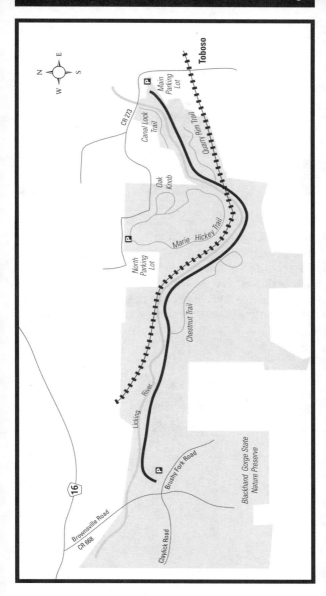

Contact and Tourist Information:

Greg Seymour
ODNR
5213 Rock Haven Road, SE
Newark, OH 43055
740-763-4411
blackhand@alltel.net

Ohio Canal Greenway

Licking

State of Project: Open
End Points: Canal Park (N) and
State Route 79 (S)
Length: 3.8 miles
Surface: Sod and cinders

This multi-purpose recreational trail is located on an old Penn Central Railroad right-of-way. Farm fields border on the west and the historic Ohio and Erie Canal borders on the east. A watered portion of the canal extends from the Hebron State Fish Hatchery to State Route 79 and is a popular area with fishing and birding enthusiasts. A genuine wooden-truss covered

bridge can be found along the trail.

Parking is available along State Route 79 and at Canal Park in Hebron.

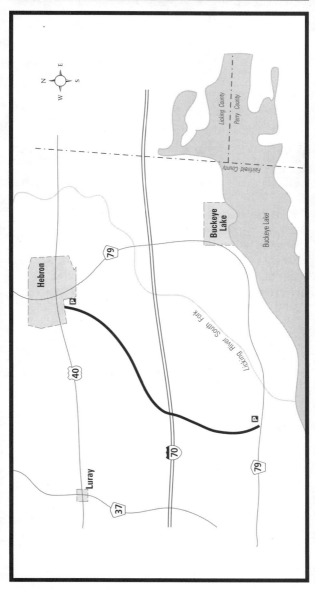

Contact and Tourist Information:

Russell Edgington
Licking Park District
P. O. Box 590
Granville, OH 43023
740-587-2535
mail@lickingparkdistrict.com
www.lickingparkdistrict.com

Thomas J. Evans Panhandle Recreational Trail

Licking

State of Project: Open
End Points: Felumlee Road (E)
and Main Street (W)
Length: 9.9 miles
Surface: Asphalt

The Panhandle Recreational Trail is a rail-with-trail that parallels active tracks of the Ohio Central Railroad, separated by a four-foot high safety fence. Beginning on the east side of downtown Newark, trail users may continue for 9.9 miles into the gently rolling and picturesque hills of eastern Licking County, passing near the unique basket-shaped Longaberger Building.

Built by the T. J. Evans Foundation, the Panhandle Trail is designed to be a key portion of the Ohio to Erie Trail (page 34), a cross-state trail that will connect Cincinnati with Cleveland through Columbus.

Parking is available at Felumee Road off of County Road 585, further west along County Road 585 in Hanover, and at the west terminus of the trail at East Main Street in Newark.

Thomas J. Evans Panhandle Recreational Trail

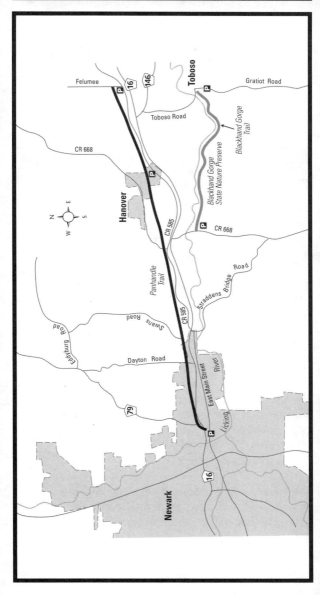

Contact and Tourist Information:

Russell Edgington
Licking Park District
P. O. Box 590
Granville, OH 43023
740-587-2535
mail@lickingparkdistrict.com

Newark Parks
and Recreation
40 West Main Street
Newark, OH 43055
740-349-6727

T. J. Evans Foundation
P. O. Box 4217
25 East Walnut Street
Newark, OH 43058
740-349-8276

Licking

State of Project: Open
End Points: Newark (E)
and Johnstown (W)
Length: 14.3 miles
Surface: Asphalt

The T. J. Evans Recreational Trail is one of the original rail-trails in Ohio. The trail begins in the village of Johnstown and continues east 14.3 miles through gently rolling farmland, skirting the historic village of Granville and continuing on into Newark where it links with the Newark trail system.

The Newark trail system also includes paths along State Route 16 with a connection to The Ohio State University at Newark, where one may find the unique Squire Whipple Cast and Wrought-Iron Bowstring Truss Bridge, built in 1872.

The T. J. Evans Recreational Trail, along with the Newark trails, will be a part of the Ohio to Erie Trail (page 34) that will connect Cincinnati with Cleveland through Columbus.

Photo: Licking County Park District

Thomas J. Evans Trail (Johnstown to Newark)

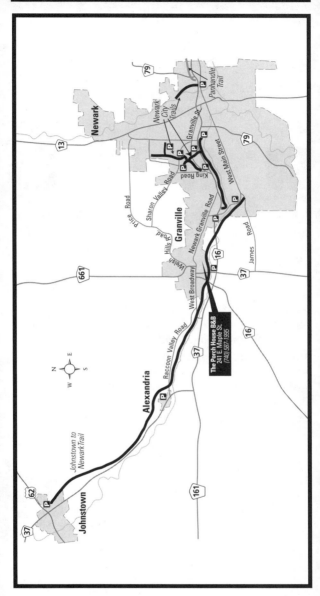

Contact and Tourist Information:

Russell Edgington
Licking Park District
P. O. Box 590
Granville, OH 43023
740-587-2535
mail@lickingparkdistrict.com

Newark Parks
& Recreation
40 West Main Street
Newark, OH 43055
740-349-6727

T. J. Evans Foundation
P. O. Box 4217
25 East Walnut Street
Newark, OH 43058
740-349-8276

Lorain

State of Project: Open
End Points: Elyria (E) and
Kipton (W)
Length: 14 miles
Surface: Asphalt

This 14-mile trail is a segment of the North Coast Inland Trail (page 30), a 65-mile trail which will eventually link Pennsylvania with Michigan and Indiana across northern Ohio.

This trail is a 12-foot wide asphalt corridor connecting the western side of Elyria to a small public park in the heart of Kipton. The city of Oberlin maintains the 3.1 miles within its city limits and the remaining part is maintained by Lorain County Metro Parks.

If visitors choose to travel the entire 14 miles between Elyria and Kipton, they will pass through historic Oberlin, home of Oberlin College.

In Kipton visitors may find parking in Kipton Park, south along Baird Road off of State Route 113. Take State Route 113 into Elyria, turn south on Lorain Boulevard to Gateway Boulevard and turn west on Third Street to the north terminus of the trail. Additional parking may be found on the street in Oberlin at State Route 58 in the downtown area.

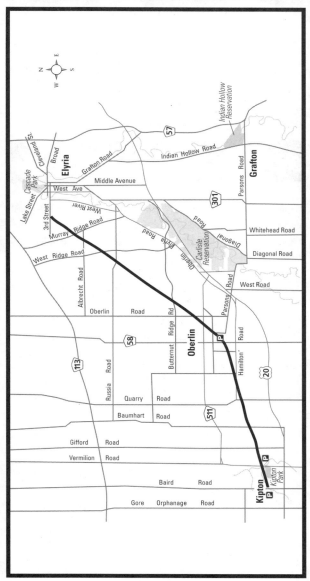

Contact and Tourist Information:

Dan Martin
Lorain County Metro Parks
12882 Diagonal Road
LaGrange, OH 44050
440-458-5121
bvoit@loraincountyparks.com
www.loraincountymetroparks.com

Lucas

State of Project: Open
End Points: University of Toledo (E) and King Road (W)
Length: 6.3 miles
Surface: Asphalt

Beginning off of King Road near Milton Olander Park and continuing to Wildwood Preserve Metropark, this trail crosses two bridges and parallels an active rail line before ending at the University of Toledo.

This trail connects with the Ottawa Park Connector on the University of Toledo campus, the Franklin Park Mall Connector along King Road, and the Wildwood Preserve Metropark on Central Avenue

Parking and trail access are available at Wildwood Preserve Metropark located at 5100 West Central Avenue, two miles east of US Route 23/Interstate 475.

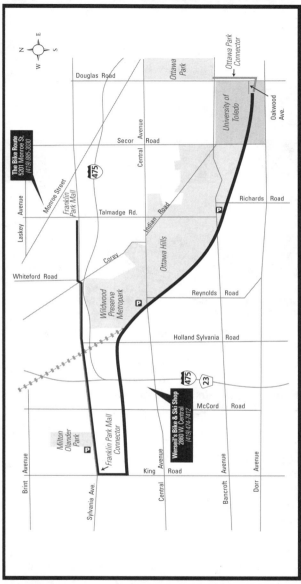

Contact and Tourist Information:

Scott Carpenter
Toledo Area Metroparks
5100 West Central Avenue
Toledo, OH 43615
419-535-3050
scott.carpenter@metroparkstoledo.com
www.metroparkstoledo.com

Mill Creek MetroParks Bikeway

Mahoning

State of Project: Open
End Points: Mahoning and Trumbull County line (N) and Western Reserve Road (S)
Length: 12 miles
Surface: Asphalt

The Mill Creek MetroParks Bikeway follows the former Conrail line that crossed through the middle of Mahoning County. Trail users will find a wide variety of scenery along the trail, including farmland, small towns, and wildlife habitat. Owned and operated by Mill Creek MetroParks, this trail is an ideal location for nature hikes, trail rides, and community events.

Mill Creek MetroParks Bikeway is one segment of the Great Ohio Lake to River Greenway (page 26).

Two trailhead areas are available for visitors to find parking and trail access. One is located at the MetroParks Farm on State Route 46 across from the Canfield Fairgrounds. A winding quarter-mile asphalt trail crossing farm fields and passing a pond provides a link from the trailhead to the main trail. Another access point is the Kirk Road Trailhead located at Kirk Road in Austintown Township, approximately mid-point along the trail.

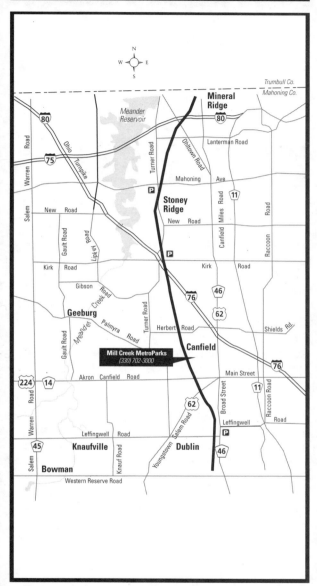

Contact and Tourist Information:

Mill Creek MetroParks
P. O. Box 596
Canfield, OH 44406
330-702-3000
www.millcreekmetroparks.com

Stavich Bicycle Trail

Mahoning (OH), Lawrence (PA)

State of Project: Open
End Points: Struthers, OH (W)
and New Castle, PA (E)
Length: 11 miles
Surface: Asphalt

The Stavich Bicycle Trail is an interstate trail that utilizes a former interurban line. There are four miles of trail in Ohio and seven miles in Pennsylvania. Unlike many rail-trails, this trail has a few hills because interurban lines had different grade requirements than freight and passenger trains.

The trail follows the scenic Mahoning River and passes through an area once booming and prosperous in the steel industry. It parallels an active rail line and encounters rolling hills, farmland, wooded countryside, and some industrial areas.

Volunteers built this trail in 1983, with funding from the John and George Stavich families and donations from local individuals. Eventually, the trail will connect with other trails in Mahoning County, including the Great Ohio Lake to River Greenway (page 26).

Parking is available in Struthers along State Route 289. In Pennsylvania parking is available in New Castle.

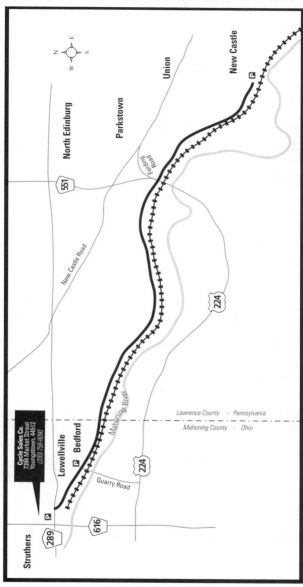

Contact and Tourist Information:

Gary Slaven
Falcon Foundry
6th and Water Streets
P.O. Box 301
Lowellville, OH 44436
330-536-6221
falcondfdry@aol.com

Medina

State of Project: Partially open
End Points: Lester Rd. (N) and Medina Community Center (S); Ryan Rd. (N) and Chippewa Rd. (S)
Length: 3.2 miles and 3.1 miles
Surface: Asphalt

The Medina County Park District is currently working on development of the Chippewa Rail Trail. The Lester Trail is complete and open.

Trail users will find scenic vistas as well as a connection with other parts of the community.

The Chippewa Trail will offer trail visitors a wooded path. The Lester Trail takes the user across State Route 252 and State Route 18 as well as several streams.

Parking is available for the open Lester Rail Trail along Lester Road. Take State Route 252 to State Route 18, turn west on State Route 18 to Lester Road, turn north, and proceed to parking facilities.

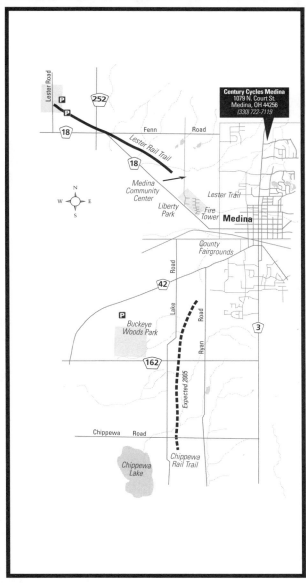

Contact and Tourist Information:

Medina County Park District
6364 Deerview Lane
Medina, OH 44256
330-722-9366
parks@medinacountyparks.com
www.medinacountyparks.com

Celina Coldwater Bikeway

Mercer

State of Project: Open
End Points: Schunck Road (N) and Vine Street (S)
Length: 4.5 miles
Surface: Asphalt

The Celina Coldwater Bikeway is an early rail-with-trail conversion from the 1980s. Long a popular trail, users follow the Penn Central Railroad between the village

of Coldwater and the city of Celina, passing near Grand Lake, the largest inland lake in Ohio.

Trail access is available at the north terminus in Celina at Schunck Road and Vine Street at the south terminus in Coldwater. Additional access is available along the route at five rural road intersections including Monroe Road, Brown Road, St. Anthony Road, Meyer Road, and Fleetfoot Road. Monroe Road and Brown Road are accessible via US Route 127 north.

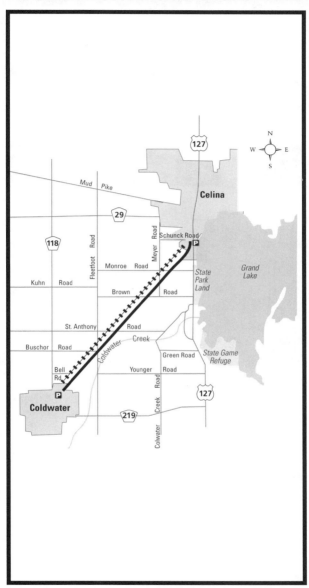

Contact and Tourist Information:

Michael Sovinski
City of Celina
426 West Market Street
Celina, OH 45822
419-586-6464
ssdir@celinaohio.org

Linear Park

Miami

State of Project: Partially open
End Points: Troy-Sidney Road (E), Spiker Road (W), French Park (S), and State Route 66 (N)
Length: 12.1 miles
Surface: Asphalt

The Linear Park follows the former Conrail right-of-way from the eastern to the western boundary of the Piqua city limits. The trail features a converted railroad bridge across the Great Miami River, spanning 535 feet, and a tunnel under Sunset Drive. The trail connects neighborhoods with a revitalized downtown area.

The Linear Park is a part of the Piqua "Loop" trail that will provide a multi-use trail route throughout the city.

Numerous Park and Ride facilities are available for trail users, including Nine Lock Park along West Water Street, and French Park at the junction of State Route 36 and State Route 66 in Piqua.

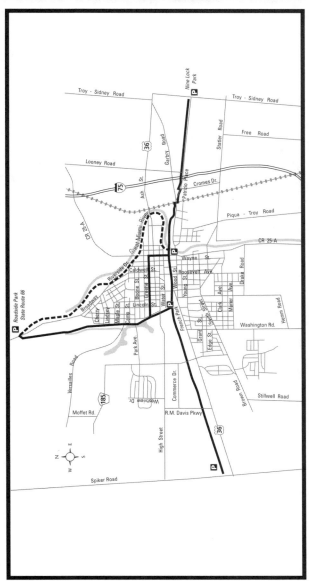

Contact and Tourist Information:

Thomas Zechman
City of Piqua
201 West Water Street
Piqua, OH 45356
937-778-2044
tzechman@piquaoh.org

Englewood Bike Trail

Montgomery

State of Project: Open
End Points: Englewood MetroPark (N) and Jake Grossnickle Memorial Park (S)
Length: 3 miles
Surface: Asphalt

The Englewood Bike Trail is a vital link in the highly urbanized north Dayton area. This three-mile asphalt trail provides a connection between Englewood Metro-Park to the north and Jake Grossnickle Park to the south. Along the way, trail users pass Samaritan North Health Center, one of the largest outpatient facilities in the nation where heart patients and others use the path in their rehabilitation regiment.

A joint project between the City of Englewood and Five Rivers MetroParks, the trail follows gently rolling land as it takes the user along the Stillwater Scenic River, under Interstate 70, and in close proximity to the Aullwood Audubon Center, one of only two national Audubon Centers.

In Englewood MetroPark, visitors will find connection with an expansive inter-park trail system. Future plans include developing a parking facility near the mid-point of the trail as well as adding picnic, restroom facilities, and landscaping along the trail.

Current parking and trail access are available in Englewood MetroPark off of US Route 40. To reach parking facilities in Jake Grossnickle Park, take State Route 48 south to Heathcliff Road, turn on to Heathcliff Road to find the park.

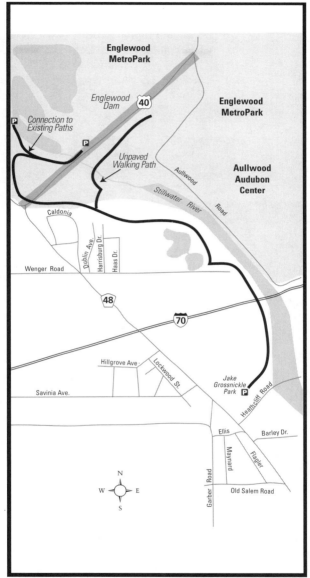

Contact and Tourist Information:

Eric A. Smith, City Manager
City of Englewood
333 West National Road
Englewood, OH 45322
937-836-5106 X 210
smith@englewood.oh.us
www.englewood.oh.us

Charlie Shoemaker, Director
Five Rivers MetroPark
1375 East Siebenthaler Avenue
Dayton, OH 45414
937-278-8231
www.metroparks.org

Iron Horse Trail

Montgomery

State of Project: Open
End Points: Hempstead Station Drive (N) and I-675 (S)
Length: 2.5 miles
Surface: Grass and dirt

The Iron Horse Trail utilizes approximately two miles of former Penn Central right-of-way, providing users a pleasant grass trail through neighborhoods as well as links with the Iron Horse Park. Future plans are to link the trail at the north terminus with the Kettering Recreation Trail.

Parking and trail access for the current two miles of trail are available at Iron Horse Park. Visitors may travel Interstate 675 to State Route 48 north, turn right on Whipp Road, and then turn right onto Millshire Drive. The entrance to the park is on the right.

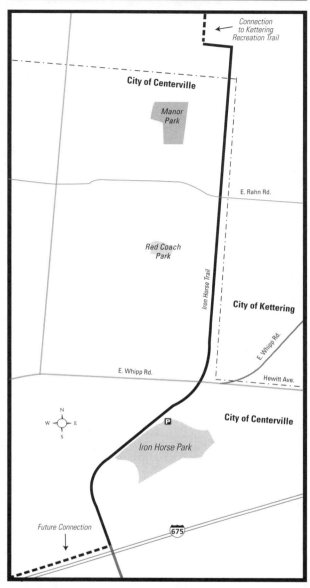

Contact and Tourist Information:

Carol Kennard, CPRP Director
Centerville-Washington Park District
221 North Main Street
Centerville, OH 45459-4617
937-433-5155
ckennard@cwpd.org
www.cwpd.org

Brian Kunkel, Park Operations Manager
Centerville-Washington Park District
221 North Main Street
Centerville, OH 45459-4617
937-433-5155
bkunkel@cwpd.org
www.cwpd.org

RT 8 / Mad River Recreation Trail

Montgomery

State of Project: Open
End Points: Eastwood MetroPark (E) and RT25/Great Miami Recreational Trail (W)
Length: 2.6 miles
Surface: Asphalt

The RT8/Mad River Recreation Trail provides a critical link between the RT2/Creekside Recreation Trail (page 98) and the RT25/Great Miami River Recreation Trail (page 46). The trail provides access from Montgomery County to the extensive trails in Greene, Warren, Clermont, and Clark Counties. This trail follows the scenic Mad River along Miami Conservancy's flood prevention levees from Eastwood MetroPark to downtown Dayton.

Parking and trail access are available at Webster Street at Corridor Drive and at the Springfield Street entrance of the Eastwood MetroPark.

Photo: www.miamivalleytrails.org

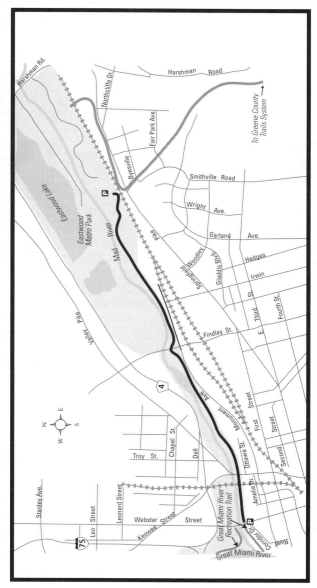

Contact and Tourist Information:

Hans Landefeld
Manager Recreation Trails
Miami Conservancy District
38 East Monument
Dayton, OH 45202-1265
937-223-1278 x3223
hlandefeld@miamiconservancy.org
www.miamiconservancy.org

Craig Wenner
Operations Manager
Five Rivers MetroParks
1375 East Siebenthaler
Dayton, OH 45414
937-278-8231
cwenner@matroparks.org
www.metroparks.org

Montgomery

State of Project: Open
End Points: Sinclair Park (N) and
            Island MetroPark (S)
Length: 3.3 miles
Surface: Asphalt

RT7/Stillwater Recreation Trail links several riverside MetroParks. The trail begins at Sinclair Park on Helena Street and crosses over the Great Miami River into Island MetroPark and winds between stands of monarch trees along the Stillwater River through DeWeese Park and Wegerzyn Gardens. DeWeese Park is the location of Boonshoft Museum of Discovery and Wegerzyn Gardens and features both formal and community gardens. The trail ends at Harrison Township's Sinclair Park off Shoup Mill Road.

Parking and trail access are available at Sinclair Park, Wegerzyn Gardens, and Island MetroPark.

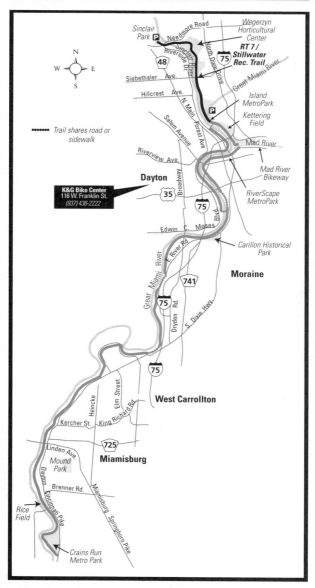

Contact and Tourist Information:

Craig Wenner, Operations Manager
Five Rivers MetroParks
1375 East Siebenthaler Avenue
Dayton, OH 45414
937-278-8231
cwenner@metroparks.org
www.metroparks.org

Eric Smith, City Manager
City of Englewood
333 West National Road
Englewood, OH 45322-1495
937-836-5106
smith@englewood.oh.us

Montgomery

State of Project: Open
End Points: Verona (N)
and Trotwood (S)
Length: 12.5 miles
Surface: Asphalt

This former Dayton and Union Railroad Company corridor went through a number of owners between its opening in 1852 and final passenger service in the 1940s.

Built by a spirit of cooperation, the RT 38/ Wolf Creek Recreation Trail connects Trotwood, Brookville, and Verona, allowing trail users to enjoy quiet fields, meadows, and woodlands. A popular location for bird watching, walking, and cycling, the trail passes by the original railroad depots in Trotwood and Brookville. These historic structures are now museums housing railroad and related memorabilia. Sycamore State Park is adjacent to the trail and has extensive bridle and hiking trails.

Parking and trail access are available along US Route 40, east of Nine Road, at Sycamore State Park along Diamond Mill Road, at Golden Gate Park in the City of Brookville, and the Trotwood Community Center near the south terminus of the trail.

Photo: www.miamivalleytrails.org

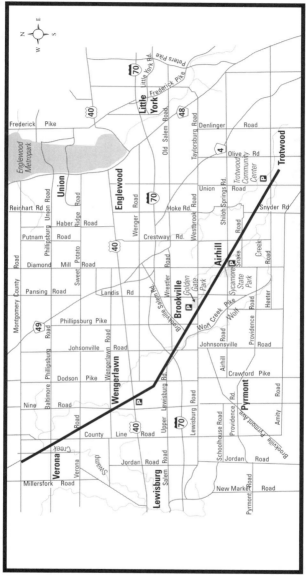

Contact and Tourist Information:

Craig Wenner, Operations Manager
Five Rivers MetroParks
1375 East Siebenthaler Avenue
Dayton, OH 45414
937-278-8231
cwenner@metroparks.org
www.metroparks.org

Muskingum Recreational Trail

Muskingum

State of Project: Partially open
End Points: Main Street (N)
and Rock Cut Road (S)
Length: 10 miles
Surface: Asphalt

The Muskingum Recreational Trail is a partially open trail that follows the Muskingum River from Zanesville to Dresden. This corridor was once the Dresden extension of the Cincinnati and Muskingum Valley Railroad that was established in 1870.

Trail users will pass by massive sandstone outcrops, farm fields, forests, and the mighty Muskingum River, which is the largest river lying solely within Ohio. The bridge over the river offers picturesque views of the Muskingum River Valley, Ellis Dam, and Lock 11.

Future plans are for the trail to join the Ohio to Erie Trail (page 34), the cross-state trail that will connect Cincinnati with Cleveland through Columbus. The link will be north of Dresden and connects Muskingum County with Licking County to the west and Coshocton County to the north.

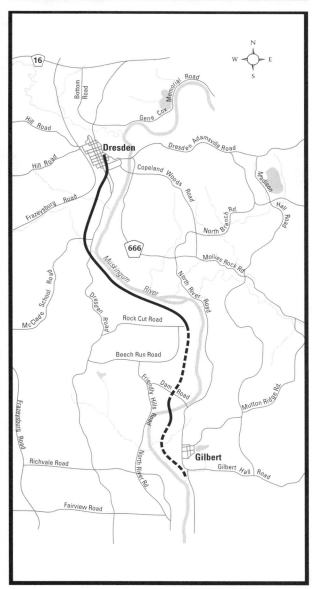

Contact and Tourist Information:

Bonnie Dailey
Muskingum Valley Park District
P. O. Box 446
Zanesville, OH 43702-0446
740-455-8237
mvpd@rrohio.com

Zane's Landing Trail

Muskingum

State of Project: Open
End Points: Riverside Park (N)
and Market Street (S)
Length: 3 miles
Surface: Asphalt

The Zane's Landing rail-with-trail follows the east branch of the Muskingum River north from Zanesville. The southern terminus is in Zane's Landing Park downtown, with the northern terminus in Riverside Park. The trail lies near the docking port of the Lorena, a paddle boat that goes along the Muskingum River, a restored trail depot, and the unique Y-Bridge just three blocks away.

Parking and trail access may be found in Riverside Park along State Route 666.

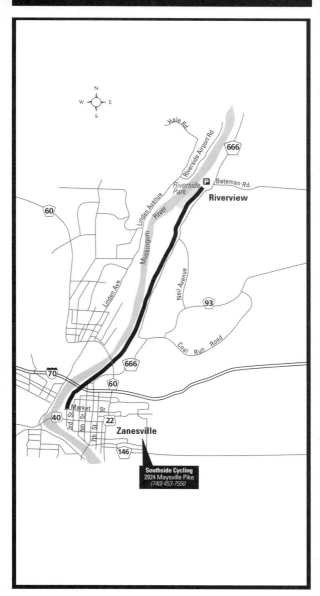

Contact and Tourist Information:

City of Zanesville
401 Market Street
Zanesville, OH 43701
740-455-0609

North Coast Inland Trail

Ottawa

State of Project: Open
End Points: Wolf Creek (SE)
and north of Witty Road (NW)
Length: 2.7 miles
Surface: Cinders

This trail follows the corridor of the Penn Central Railroad that once served the communities from Cleveland to Toledo. Crossing the Portage River and Sugar Creek, it offers scenic views and recreational opportunities for residents and visitors for walking, cycling, and wildlife observation. It also links downtown Elmore with schools, residences, and green spaces.

This trail is a link in the North Coast Inland Trail (page 30), a trail that will link Pennsylvania with Michigan and Indiana across northern Ohio.

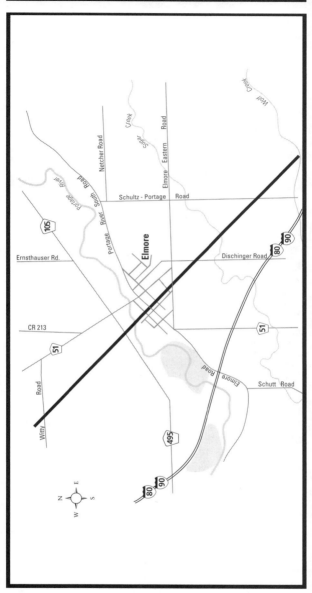

Contact and Tourist Information:

Village of Elmore
340 Clinton Street, Box 1
Elmore, OH 43416
419-862-3454

The Headwaters Trail

Portage

State of Project: Open
End Points: Garrettsville (E)
and Mantua (W)
Length: 7 miles
Surface: Crushed limestone

The trail utilizes the former Erie Lackawana Railroad corridor from Mennonite Road in historic Mantua Village, east to historic Garrettsville Village. It crosses the Cuyahoga River in Manuta, and then passes by the Berdena Marsh and Mantua Bog State Nature Preserves. The trail continues across the divide of the Lake Erie and Ohio River watersheds, to the site of the former Jeddoe Station in Hiram, ending in Garrettsville at the Village Park, approximately three miles west of Eagle Creek State Nature Preserve. Plans are for an additional mile to be completed in the summer of 2005.

Trailhead parking is available at Manuta Village Park on High Street by the Cuyahoga River, on State Route 700 in Hiram and at Garrettsville Village Park on State Route 88 in Garrettsville.

Photo: Ian Adams

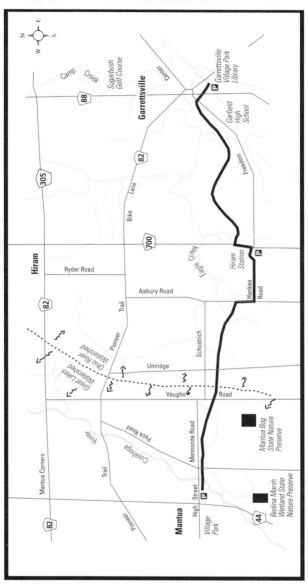

Contact and Tourist Information:

Christine Craycroft
Portage Park District
128 North Prospect Street
Ravenna, OH 44226
330-297-7728
www.portageparkdistrict.org

The Portage Hike and Bike Trail

Portage

State of Project: Open
End Points: Chestnut Hills Park (E),
Judson Rd (W), and Lake Rockwell Rd
Length: 20 miles
Surface: Asphalt and
crushed limestone

The Portage Hike and Bike Trail currently offers trail users approximately 6.5 miles of a planned 20 miles. Five miles are available along the Towner's Woods section of the trail from Lake Rockwell Road to Chestnut Hills Park. This section of the trail passes by prairie, woods, and wetlands, and is often used for nature appreciation as well as hiking and biking. It is a crushed limestone surface between the City of Ravenna and Franklin Township, with two miles of the trail being a rail-with-trail along an active railroad line that sees a few trains a week.

Future plans include connections to the City of Kent and Kent State University to the west, and the county line to the east, eventually forming an east-west connector across Portage County between north-south trails of the Great Ohio Lake to River Greenway (page 26) and the Ohio and Erie Canalway Towpath Trail (page 70). Trailhead parking is currently available at Beckwith's Orchards on Lake Rockwell Road, Towner's Woods Park on Ravenna Road, and Cleveland Road Ravenna.

The Franklin Connector Trail section of The Portage Hike and Bike Trail will be open by the end of the year 2004. This 1.5-mile trail segment will eventually serve as a link with the Summit County Hike and Bike Trail (page 184) operated by Metro Parks Serving Summit County.

Parking for this trail segment is available on Judson Road.

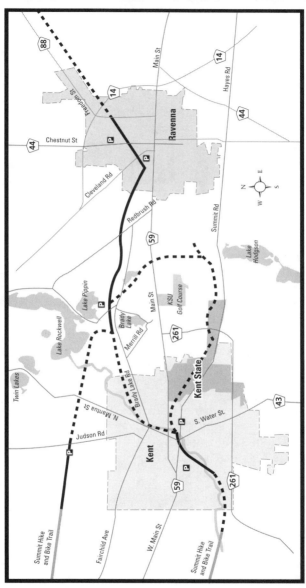

Contact and Tourist Information:

Christine Craycroft
Portage Park District
128 North Prospect Street
Ravenna, OH 44226
330-297-7728
www.portageparkdistrict.org

Richland B&O Trail

Richland

State of Project: Open
End Points: Northlake Park (N)
and Hitchman Park (S)
Length: 18.4 miles
Surface: Asphalt

The Richland B&O rail-trail utilizes the former Baltimore & Ohio Railroad corridor through the towns of Butler, Bellville, Lexington, and Mansfield. The trail, which goes through picturesque farmland and rolling hills, starts in Butler near the Clear Fork Ski Area and Malabar Farm State Park. The path follows the Clear Fork of the Mohican River to Lexington. In Lexington, the path passes near a county park, the Gorman Nature Center, and the Richland County Historical Society. The trail continues north to Mansfield, ending next to North Lake Park. A footbridge connects the trail with the park. Be aware that the steps may prevent wheelchair use.

This trail is a part of the Heart of Ohio Trail System (page 28) and will eventually connect with the Kokosing Gap Trail (page 124), nine miles away, the Mohican Valley Trail (page 126), and the Holmes County Trail (page 118), at the southern terminus.

Parking is available at the north terminus of the trail at North Lake Park in Mansfield. Heading south, additional parking is available at the junction of the trail at Millsboro Road, at Deer Park on Home Road on the southwest side of Mansfield. In Lexington, parking is at Community Park; watch for signs along Plymouth Street just north of the village square. If traveling along Interstate 71, access the trail and parking half a mile east of exit 165, at the junction of the trail and State Route 97. In Bellville, there is parking both on Ogle Street and at the restored Village Train Depot just west of Main Street. At the south terminus of the trail, find parking at Hitchman Park.

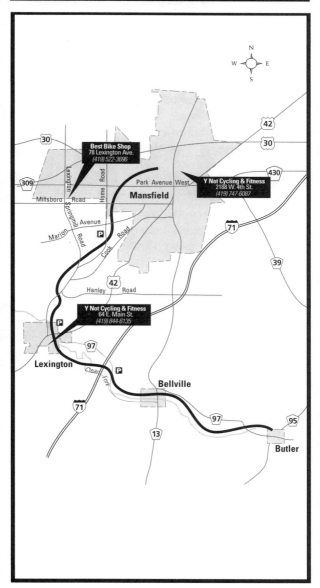

Contact and Tourist Information:

Steve McKee
Richland County Park District
2295 Lexington Avenue
Mansfield, OH 44907
419-884-3764
smmckee52@hotmail.com

Mansfield Tourist/Vistitors Bureau
124 North Main Street
Mansfield, OH 44902
419-525-1300
visitors@mansfieldtourism.com

North Coast Inland Trail – Clyde to Fremont

Sandusky

State of Project: Open
End Points: Clyde (E) and
 Fremont (W)
Length: 6.5 miles
Surface: Asphalt

This segment of the North Coast Inland Trail (page 30) utilizes the former Toledo, Norwalk and Cleveland Railroad that was established in 1851 as the final link in a direct New York to Chicago rail corridor. Many of the villages along the corridor owe their existence to the railroad. The line remained active until the 1970s.

From Clyde to Fremont in Sandusky County, the asphalt trail segment has been open as a rail-with-trail since 1997. The trail is separated from the active rail line by water and trees, crosses Green Creek, and ends near the Biggs-Kettner Park in Fremont.

Parking and trail access are available at Biggs-Kettner Park in Fremont. Take US Route 20 south to East State Street, turn west to St. Joseph Road, and proceed to the Biggs-Kettner Park.

North Coast Inland Trail – Clyde to Fremont

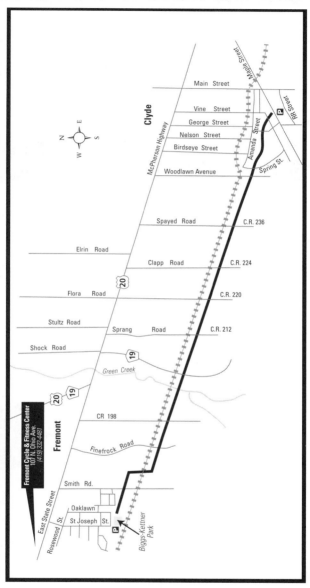

Contact and Tourist Information:

Steve Gruner, Director
Sandusky County Park District
1970 Countryside Place
Fremont, OH 43420
419-334-4495
steve@scpd-parks.org
www.scpd-parks.org

Nickleplate Trail

Stark

State of Project: Open
End Points: Pinevale Avenue (E) and
South Chapel Street (W)
Length: 2.5 miles
Surface: Asphalt

The Nickleplate Trail lies at the edge of Metzger Park between South Chapel Street and Pinevale Avenue. It connects to a network of smaller paths inside Metzger Park to create several different loops. Each is marked with a color-coded arrow to assist the visitor through the park.

Parking and trail access are available at the east trail terminus at Pinevale Avenue.

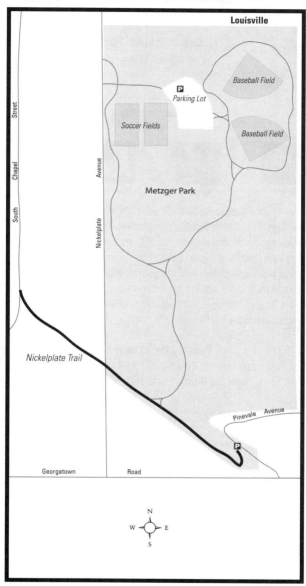

Contact and Tourist Information:

Stark Parks
5360 Tyner Street NW
Canton, OH 44708
330-477-3552

Stark Electric Railway Trail

Stark

State of Project: Partially open
End Points: Kirby Avenue NE (E) and
Hilcher Avenue NE (W)
Length: 33 miles
Surface: Limestone and concrete

The Stark Electric Railway Trail is a former interurban rail line that ran from Canton to Salem via Louisville, Alliance, and Sebring from 1902 to July 15, 1939. The railroad was nicknamed the "Bachelor Railroad" because most of its executives were unmarried. Through the 1930s the line was busy, but buses were less expensive to operate and the train eventually ceased operation.

In 2001, the Stark County Park District constructed the first one-mile segment of trail between Hilcher and Kirby Avenue along State Route 153.

Parking is available along Mahoning Road NE.

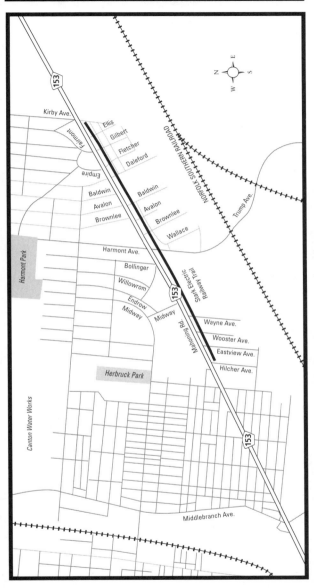

Contact and Tourist Information:

Connie Rubin
Public Relations Coordinator
Stark County Park District
5300 Tyner Street NW
Canton, OH 44708
330-477-3552
info@starkparks.com
www.starkparks.com

Joe Concatto
Chief of Staff for
the Mayor City of Canton
218 Cleveland Avenue SW
Canton, OH 44702
330-489-3087
jjconcat@ci.canton.oh.us
www.cityofcanton.com

Doug Perry, Director
Canton City Parks
Department
2436 30th Street NE
Canton, OH 44705
330-489-3015
cantonparks@ci.canton.oh.us
www.cityofcanton.com

Sippo Valley Trail

Stark, Wayne

State of Project: Open
End Points: Bottoms Park in Massillon (E) and Village Green Park in Dalton (W)
Length: 10.5 miles
Surface: Asphalt and crushed limestone

The Sippo Valley Trail connects Bottoms Park in Massillon, Stark County, to Village Green Park in Dalton, Wayne County. The trail follows the former rail bed of the Wheeling and Lake Erie Railroad. Service began on this line in 1881, with limited service continuing until 1994. The rail bed was acquired and then donated to the City of Massillon for this trail.

Bottoms Park in Massillon is located off of Sixth Street and Water Street just before the west end of the bridge over the Tuscarawas River. Asphalt surface extends from the park to just short of State Route 93. The trail continues with a crushed limestone surface to the Wayne County line at Deerfield Avenue. After crossing the county line at Deerfield Avenue, the trail is again asphalt surface into Village Green Park in Dalton.

A one-mile connector trail that also utilizes off-trail facilities provides the user with access to the Ohio & Erie Canalway Towpath Trail (page 70) at Walnut Run. Follow on-street signage for the route.

Parking is available along the trail at West Lebanon Road in Wayne County. Travel east on US Route 30 to West Lebanon Road and turn north.

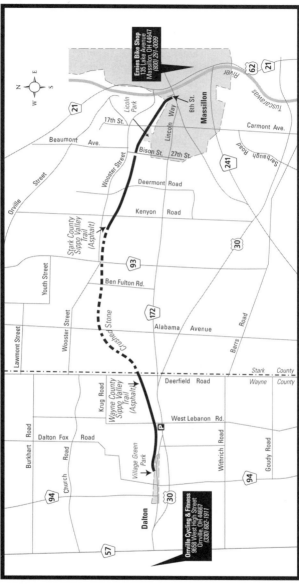

Contact and Tourist Information:

Keith Workman, Trustee
Rails-to-Trails of Wayne County
2786 Chippewa Road
Orrville, OH 44667
330-682-7188
kcw2786@copper.net
www.railtotrailsofwaynecounty.org
www.sippovalleytrail.org

Ernie Lehman, Trustee
Massillon Area Greenways Inc.
C/O Chamber of Commerce
137 E. Lincolnway, Massillon, OH 44646
800-291-0099
ernie@erniesbikeshop.com
www.erniesbikeshop.com

Bike and Hike Trail

Summit, Cuyahoga, Portage

State of Project: Open
End Points: Walton Hills (N),
Kent (SW), and Stow (SE)
Length: 32 miles
Surface: Asphalt and
          crushed limestone

The scenic beauty of the Bike and Hike Trail has been delighting users since 1972. Ohio's second rail-trail, the trail utilizes the former Akron, Bedford and Cleveland (AB&C) Railroad, which was the longest electric railroad of its kind when it began operation in 1895. Some of the trail also uses former New York Central Railroad corridor.

The trail intersects the Cuyahoga River; the Silver, Wyoga, and Crystal Lakes; Virginia Kendall Parks; and Brandywine Falls.

Parking is available at Silver Springs Park in Stow, along Darrow Road in Kent, and along Akron Cleveland Road just south of Route 303.

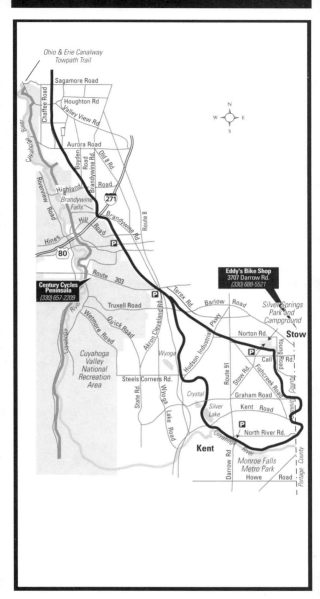

Contact and Tourist Information:

Metro Parks Serving Summit County
975 Treaty Line Road
Akron, OH 44313
330-867-5511
www.summitmetroparks.org

Trumbull

State of Project: Planned
End Points: Niles (N) and Mill Creek
MetroParks Bikeway (S)
Length: 4.9 miles
Surface: Asphalt

This nearly five-mile segment of the Great Ohio Lake to River Greenway (page 26) is expected to be constructed in two phases. The first phase is scheduled for construction during the summer of 2005. This four-mile trail will link the Niles Greenway with the 11-mile Mill Creek MetroParks Bikeway (page 144) at the Trumbull and Mahoning County line. The second phase, nine-tenths of a mile, will continue to Niles City corporate limits to the north.

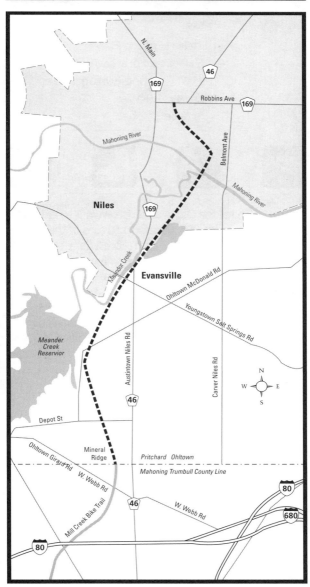

Contact and Tourist Information:

Alan Knapp, Director
Trumbull County
Planning Commission
347 North Park Avenue
Warren, OH 44481
330-675-2480
pcknapp@co.trumbull.oh.us

Mark Hess
Engineering and Grant
Development Coordinator
City of Niles Department
of Engineering
34 West State Street
Niles, OH 44446
330-544-9000 ext. 181
mhess@thecityofniles.com

Alex Bobersky, Volunteer
Great Ohio Lake to River
Greenway Coalition
646 Tod Avenue, NW
Warren, OH 44485
330-393-9439
www.greenway.co.trumbull.oh.us

Old Warren Bikeway

Trumbull

State of Project: Planned
End Points: Forest Street (N)
and Burton Street (S)
Length: 1.9 miles
Surface: Asphalt

Construction for the Old Warren Bikeway is scheduled for the summer of 2005, utilizing 1.9 miles of the former Baltimore and Ohio rail line from Forest Street to High Street. From High Street, trail users will need to follow Charles Avenue to South Street, where the former rail line picks up and continues for approximately 600 feet south to the southern city corporation limits near Burton Street. Future plans call for the Old Warren Bikeway to link with the planned 2.5-mile Niles-Warren Link trail at this point, continuing the Great Ohio Lake to River Greenway (page 26).

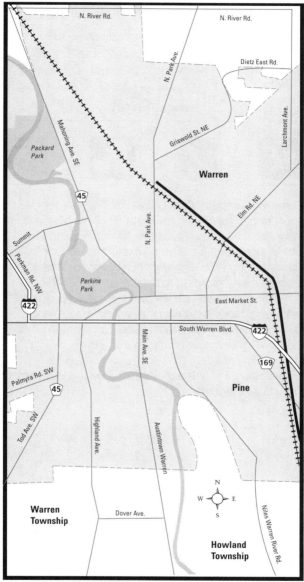

Contact and Tourist Information:

Alan Knapp, Director
Trumbull County
Planning Commission
347 North Park Avenue
Warren, OH 44481
330-675-2480
pcknapp@co.trumbull.oh.us

Alex Bobersky, Volunteer
Great Ohio Lake To River
Greenway Coalition
646 Tod Avenue, NW
Warren, OH 44485
330-393-9439
www.greenway.co.trumbull.oh.us

Bill Totten
Engineering
City of Warren
540 Laird Avenue, SE
Warren, OH 44484
330-841-2653

Marietta Bike Trail

Washington

State of Project: Partially open
End Points: State Route 821 (N) and
Downtown Marietta (S)
Length: 6 miles
Surface: Asphalt

Three miles of this trail are available. The trail begins at the Marietta Harbor on the east side of the Muskingum River. From there the trailheads upstream along the Muskingum River and into Muskingum Park. The trail passes through the park and then leaves the river for a short portion, returning to the river at the Washington Street Bridge. It then passes near the museum, continues along the river to Sacra Via Park, follows Allen Street, and then heads back to the river crossing Clark Run through the county fairgrounds.

Future plans are for the trail to continue at Indian Acres Park and continue north.

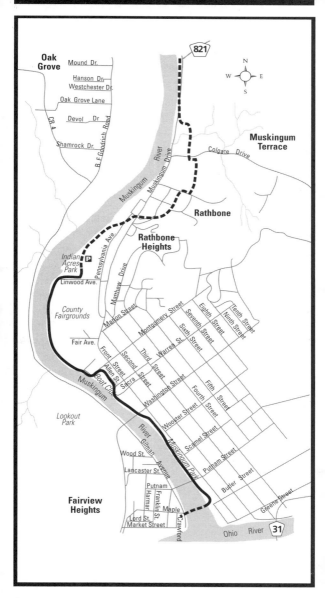

Contact and Tourist Information:

Michael Gulliver
City of Marietta
Development Department
304 Putnam Street
Marietta, OH 45750

North Coast Inland Trail – Wabash Connector

Wood

State of Project: Partially open
End Points: Millbury (E)
and Walbridge (W)
Length: 12 miles
Surface: Asphalt

The 1.9-mile asphalt trail segment is the first phase of what will be a 12-mile link between the North Coast Inland Trail (page 30) and the Wabash Cannonball Trail (page 92).

Currently, there is a 4.1-mile bike route from Millbury Road in Millbury via Ayers Road to Drouillard Road, where the on-road path intersects the existing 1.9-mile bike path that runs north and south along the west side of Drouillard Road, connecting Lake Township Park and the downtown area of the Village of Walbridge.

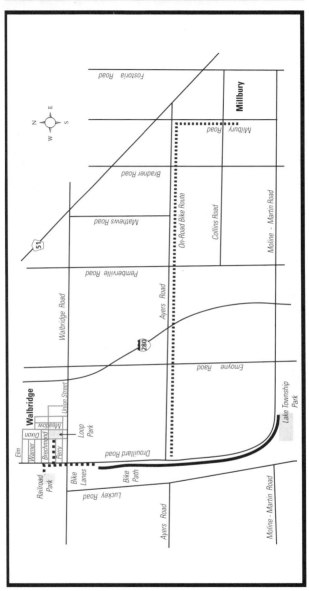

Contact and Tourist Information:

Neil Munger, Director
Wood County Park District
18729 Mercer Road
Bowling Green, OH 43402
419-353-1897
email@woodcountyparkdistrict.org
www.woodcountyparkdistrict.org

Slippery Elm Trail

Wood

State of Project: Open
End Points: Bowling Green (N)
and North Baltimore (S)
Length: 13 miles
Surface: Asphalt

The Slippery Elm Trail is named for the trees that were used to build a railroad from Tontogany to Bowling Green. The Bowling Green Railroad Company was organized in 1874. In 1891, the line was extended to North Baltimore. In 1973, after 103 year of service, the line was discontinued.

The Slippery Elm Trail utilizes the corridor from Bowling Green to North Baltimore, offering the trail user a 13-mile route through farmland, green meadows, wooded

areas, and the last remainder of the Great Black Swamp. The trail also has a grass berm suitable for horses.

Parking and trail access are available

at designated points along the trail including the north terminus at Sand Ridge Road, Gypsy Lake Road, the Portage Road Intersection, at the Liberty Township Hall in the Village of Rudolph, and at the south terminus in North Baltimore.

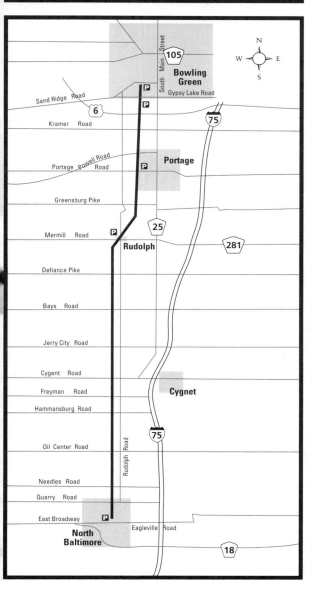

Contact and Tourist Information:

Neil Munger, Director
Wood County Park District
18729 Mercer Road
Bowling Green, OH 43402
419-353-1897
email@woodcountyparkdistrict.org
www.woodcountyparkdistrict.org